ASP.NET 8 Best Practices

Explore techniques, patterns, and practices to
develop effective large-scale .NET web apps

Jonathan R. Danylko

BIRMINGHAM—MUMBAI

ASP.NET 8 Best Practices

Group Product Manager: Rohit Rajkumar

Publishing Product Manager: Jane D'Souza

Senior Editor: Aamir Ahmed

Book Project Manager: Sonam Pandey

Technical Editor: Simran Ali

Copy Editor: Safis Editing

Proofreader: Safis Editing

Indexer: Manju Arasan

Production Designer: Prashant Ghare

DevRel Marketing Coordinator: Nivedita Pandey

First published: December 2023

Production reference: 1011223

Published by Packt Publishing Ltd.

Grosvenor House

11 St Paul's Square

Birmingham

B3 1RB, UK

ISBN 978-1-83763-212-1

www.packtpub.com

To my family, for their continued support throughout my career
(even though I tend to live in the office).

To my colleagues and mentors: this book is a culmination of our discussions, experiences, and
solutions (and some fires) we've encountered over the years.

To my readers and supporters on DanylkoWeb.com, who allow me to turn their questions into blog
posts to further everyone's knowledge in the end.

Finally, to my parents, who bought me that Commodore VIC-20 when I was 11, which started me on
my journey of building software.

–Jonathan

Contributors

About the author

Jonathan R. Danylko is an award-winning web architect who works at Insight, an international company providing enterprise-level solutions. He started development at age 11 with a Commodore VIC-20. He has competed in international programming competitions and has contributed to various publications as an author and technical editor. His career spans 25 years of building internet and intranet websites for small, medium, and Fortune 500 companies, since 1996. He also created, developed, and maintains a blog called DanylkoWeb.com and has been writing blog posts since 2006. Jonathan continues to write code on a daily basis in his personal and professional career.

About the reviewers

Matthew D. Groves is a guy who loves to code. It doesn't matter whether it's C#, jQuery, or PHP: he'll submit pull requests for anything. He has been coding professionally ever since he wrote a QuickBASIC point-of-sale app for his parent's pizza shop back in the 90s. He currently works for Couchbase, helping developers in any way he can. His free time is spent with his family, watching the Reds, and getting involved in the developer community. He is the author of *AOP in .NET*, co-author of Pro *Microservices in .NET*, a Pluralsight author, and a Microsoft MVP.

Abdulkabir Abdulwasiu is a dedicated individual from Nigeria, holding a bachelor's degree in mathematics and education. My journey led me to the Federal University of Technology Minna, honing my skills in this specialization. Further education at Nigeria Defense Academy earned me a post-graduate diploma in computer science, igniting my passion for its dynamic potential.

As a classroom teacher for over four years, I've inspired young minds through math education. In 2021, I began a software developer role at Vatebra Limited, driving tech innovation in Nigeria. Proficient in C# and .NET, I leverage technology for positive change.

My commitment to learning extends beyond teaching and coding. As a research assistant with Ph.D. students, I explore uncharted territories, refining my research skills. This journey encapsulates my dedication to growth and contributing to cutting-edge academia.

I would like to express my gratitude to my mentors, colleagues, and family for their unwavering support. Their guidance has been invaluable in shaping my journey as an educator, researcher, and software developer. Their belief in my potential has inspired me to reach new heights, and for that, I am truly thankful.

Table of Contents

3

Best Approaches for Middleware   39

4

Applying Security from the Start   55

5

Optimizing Data Access with Entity Framework Core   77

6

Best Practices with Web User Interfaces   99

7

Testing Your Code   127

8

Catching Exceptions with Exception Handling   143

9

Creating Better Web APIs   157

10

Push Your Application with Performance   179

11

Appendix   207

Preface

Welcome to *ASP.NET 8 Best Practices*!

ASP.NET 8 Best Practices contains over 100 best practices used in the ASP.NET community, covering topics such as how to squeeze the best performance out of your ASP.NET web application, what Entity Framework patterns are available, how to design a minimal web API, and how to structure Visual Studio projects based on project type.

The standards covered in the book include version control, creating software pipelines, creating structured middleware, security practices, Entity Framework Core patterns and techniques, and automating time-consuming client-side tasks.

We'll also look at common practices when testing your code, when and how to apply exception handling, how to design the best API for web applications, how to optimize a web application for performance, and finally, review common terms and guidelines when building ASP.NET web applications.

While best practices are considered recommendations on how to write professional code, there will always be exceptions to the rule. As developers know, there are so many ways to write code to achieve the same result. Some ways are better than others. These "better ways" are what I consider best practices.

As we cover each topic, we'll provide as much detail and referral material to explain why these techniques and patterns are indeed a better way to write professional code. However, it doesn't mean they are written in stone. As mentioned previously, there will always be exceptions to the rule.

To new developers entering the ASP.NET ecosystem, it can be overwhelming to build a new ASP.NET website and see everything associated with the process. This book is meant to lessen the feeling of being overwhelmed by understanding each technology "spoke" attached to an ASP.NET website "hub." It explores everything involved in creating a "simple" website.

To seasoned developers already using ASP.NET, use this book as a reference for recommendations and the observations I've gathered over a 20-year career. Even my experiences with past and present colleagues are included in this book.

Who this book is for

This book is for developers who have a working knowledge of ASP.NET and want to pursue their careers by learning best practices in a developer community or corporate environment. While there may be subjects new to you, this book can be used as a reference to gain more clarity on an ASP.NET topic at any time. After finishing the book, you will have a better understanding of the common practices used throughout the industry, whether you're a solo developer or work in a Fortune 500 company on a team.

What this book covers

Chapter 1, *Taking Control with Source Control*, addresses why source control is important, identifying and selecting a branching workflow, why tags are important, and proper commit etiquette.

Chapter 2, *CI/CD – Building Quality Software Automatically*, defines what CI/CD is, understanding and preparing code for a pipeline along with identifying two "falling" approaches when errors appear, how to deploy databases, and the various types of CI/CD providers, such as Azure, AWS, and Google Cloud Platform.

Chapter 3, *Best Approaches for Middleware*, explains what middleware is and how to optimize a middleware pipeline, using request delegates and extension methods, along with building an example middleware component.

Chapter 4, *Applying Security from the Start*, covers why security should be a top concern before, during, and after writing code, as well as common security practices. The chapter concludes by addressing the top three security threats on the internet.

Chapter 5, *Optimizing Data Access with Entity Framework Core*, looks at the different types of implementations of Entity Framework and how each one is used, why logging and async/await is important, how to use resources for large seed data, and why sometimes it's better to bypass LINQ and use stored procedures.

Chapter 6, *Best Practices for Web User Interfaces*, examines what a task runner is, why they're important, and how to create a workflow using one, along with reviewing UI standards such as centralizing site URLs, why controllers/pages should be small, why `ViewComponents` are beneficial, and how to create SEO-friendly URLs.

Chapter 7, *Testing Your Code*, explains the various types of testing concepts used in ASP.NET applications, why writing unit tests is important, why "100% test coverage" isn't necessary, how to properly structure your unit tests with the triple-A approach (AAA), when to avoid writing extra unit test helpers, and how to use tests as documentation.

Chapter 8, *Catching Exceptions with Exception Handling*, reviews the different types of exception handling, how and when to use exception handling, and using global exception handling.

It also covers logging, how unit testing and exceptional handling are similar, why empty try..catch blocks are wasteful, how to use exception filtering and pattern matching, and knowing when to use finally blocks.

Chapter 9, Creating Better Web APIs, demonstrates various practical API techniques, such as designing, creating, and testing APIs quickly, along with applying the right HTTP verbs and status codes to an API, how to implement a pagination structure, versioning, and DTOs into your APIs, and why creating a new `HttpClient` should be avoided.

Chapter 10, Push Your Application with Performance, takes everything we've learned throughout the chapters and applies a performance perspective to it. We'll cover why performance is so important and why it matters, how to establish client, C# code, and database baselines, along with image optimization, minimizing requests, using CDNs, implementing async/await, how to automatically optimize HTML, Entity Framework Core optimizations, and caching strategies.

Appendix, will review the fundamental terms used throughout the industry, such as the DRY, YAGNI, KISS principles, along with separation of concerns, how to refactor code, understanding the SOLID principles, and how to structure various project types in Visual Studio.

To get the most out of this book

You will need a version of Visual Studio for the code presented throughout the book. You should have a general knowledge of how to use Visual Studio and understand how to open solutions and debugging applications.

Software/hardware covered in the book	Operating system requirements
Visual Studio 2022 (any version) or favorite IDE supporting .NET 8	Windows, macOS, or Linux
Git (optional)	Windows, macOS, or Linux
SQL Server Management Studio (version 16 or higher)	Windows

If you are using the digital version of this book, we advise you to type the code yourself or access the code from the book's GitHub repository (a link is available in the next section). Doing so will help you avoid any potential errors related to the copying and pasting of code.

The ideal developer setup for the book is to have Visual Studio 2022 Enterprise, Git, and SQL Server Management Studio already installed.

Download the example code files

You can download the example code files for this book from GitHub at `https://github.com/PacktPublishing/ASP.NET-8-Best-Practices`. If there's an update to the code, it will be updated in the GitHub repository.

We also have other code bundles from our rich catalog of books and videos available at https://github.com/PacktPublishing/. Check them out!

Conventions used

There are a number of text conventions used throughout this book.

Code in text: Indicates code words in text, database table names, folder names, filenames, file extensions, pathnames, dummy URLs, user input, and Twitter handles. Here is an example: "A better approach would be using the newest TryParse with var, as shown here."

A block of code is set as follows:

```
var number = "2";
if (!int.TryParse(number, out var result))
{
    result = 0;
}
// use result
```

Bold: Indicates a new term, an important word, or words that you see on screen. For instance, words in menus or dialog boxes appear in **bold**. Here is an example: "Uncheck the **Use Controllers** option to use minimal APIs."

> **Tips or important notes**
> Appear like this.

Get in touch

Feedback from our readers is always welcome.

General feedback: If you have questions about any aspect of this book, email us at customercare@packtpub.com and mention the book title in the subject of your message.

Errata: Although we have taken every care to ensure the accuracy of our content, mistakes do happen. If you have found a mistake in this book, we would be grateful if you would report this to us. Please visit www.packtpub.com/support/errata and fill in the form.

Piracy: If you come across any illegal copies of our works in any form on the internet, we would be grateful if you would provide us with the location address or website name. Please contact us at copyright@packtpub.com with a link to the material.

If you are interested in becoming an author: If there is a topic that you have expertise in and you are interested in either writing or contributing to a book, please visit authors.packtpub.com.

Share Your Thoughts

Once you've read *ASP.NET 8 Best Practices*, we'd love to hear your thoughts! Scan the QR code below to go straight to the Amazon review page for this book and share your feedback.

https://packt.link/r/1-837-63480-7

Your review is important to us and the tech community and will help us make sure we're delivering excellent quality content.

Download a free PDF copy of this book

Thanks for purchasing this book!

Do you like to read on the go but are unable to carry your print books everywhere? Is your eBook purchase not compatible with the device of your choice?

Don't worry, now with every Packt book you get a DRM-free PDF version of that book at no cost.

Read anywhere, any place, on any device. Search, copy, and paste code from your favorite technical books directly into your application.

The perks don't stop there, you can get exclusive access to discounts, newsletters, and great free content in your inbox daily

Follow these simple steps to get the benefits:

1.   Scan the QR code or visit the link below

https://packt.link/free-ebook/978-1-83763-212-1

2.   Submit your proof of purchase

3.   That's it! We'll send your free PDF and other benefits to your email directly

1

Taking Control with Source Control

Source control is a developer's best friend and provides them with a way to experiment with code without losing important changes. Source control is the ability to track and maintain changes made to code throughout a development process. While this could include code, it can also be used for documentation, assets (such as images), and other resources. Being able to test certain conditions and the ability to refactor code without worrying about the code base is what most developers consider a superpower.

Source control is extremely important when working in a team environment. If a developer checks in code and later realizes they made a mistake, source control gives developers a way to revert changes or update a branch and re-commit. Companies not using some type of source control almost always raises a red flag.

In this chapter, we'll look at common practices developers use in the industry when using source control. We'll also cover various ways to implement branching workflows for your code as well as examine the different types of branches in each workflow. To finish off the chapter, we'll review common etiquette among developers when using source control.

In this chapter, we're going to cover the following topics:

- Branching Strategies
- Creating short-lived branches
- Always "Get Latest" Before Committing
- Understanding Common Practices

By the end of this chapter, you'll have learned the best approach to creating a repository of your code in an organized fashion, along with common guidelines in the developer community.

Technical requirements

While this section touches on a number of guidelines regarding source control, the only requirement for this chapter is a computer with any OS. Git is optional.

If you don't have Git installed, you can download and install it at the following URL:

```
https://git-scm.com/
```

We have used mermaid-js to visually show the branching strategies. As of February 2022, GitHub pages now support Mermaid-js. Some of the sections will include mermaid diagrams to demonstrate the different branching hierarchies.

For more information on Mermaid-js, navigate to the following URL:

```
https://mermaid-js.github.io
```

Branching Strategies

In this section, we'll explore various branching strategies, explaining how each one works, and highlighting the differences between them.

While every company has its unique workflow, we'll focus on some commonly used strategies in the industry.

With GitFlow being the initial workflow, everyone is familiar with it in the industry and its successors have improved by making minor changes to the workflow.

In the next sections, we'll discuss each workflow, but first, we have to understand the fundamentals of GitFlow.

GitFlow

One of the most common and most mature workflows in the industry is GitFlow. It was created by *Vincent Driessen* in 2010.

A minimal Git repository should have the following branches:

- main/master/trunk (referred to as main from this point on)
- develop

The `main` branch is what you start with when creating a new repository. The purpose of this branch is to *always* have stable and production-ready code for release at any time.

The `develop` branch is for writing new code and preventing untested code from being merged into `main`.

If you're a standalone developer working on a side project, this may be a suitable workflow. If everything works in `develop`, you merge your changes into `main` and deploy your first version.

The good news is you can evolve your branching hierarchy even further. You can easily create additional branches, such as feature, release, or hotfix branches, for a better workflow, which we'll cover later.

Keep in mind that each branching workflow discussed as follows allows any team, whether it's 1 developer or 50 developers, to have a solid understanding of GitFlow.

In any source control system, there are usually three types of branches used to assist with managing a software workflow: feature, release, and hotfix branches.

Feature Branches

Feature branching isolates a new feature into a single branch so a developer can write code without worrying about affecting the core code in the `develop` branch.

In the following example (see *Figure 1.1*), a team created a GitHub repository. It called its primary branch `main` and the development branch `develop`.

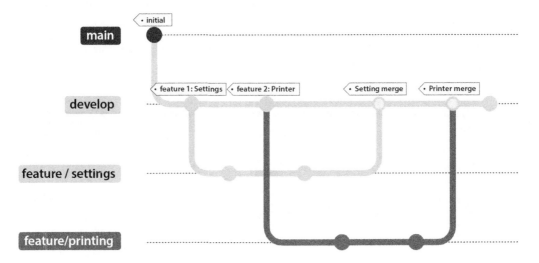

Figure 1.1: Feature branches in GitFlow

Once everyone received their tasks, one developer was assigned to create the **Settings** feature. He created a branch called `feature/settings` from the `develop` branch.

Another developer was assigned the **Printing** feature and created a `feature/printing` branch also from the `develop` branch.

> ### Naming Branches
>
> Apart from the standardized main and develop branches, one common way to name branches is to prefix the names. Some examples include the following:
>
> * `feature/`, `features/`, or `feature-`: The branch name should be as descriptive and helpful as possible. For example, `feature/1234-settings` relates to the **Settings feature** and includes a task number to reference for possible requirements. Another common method is to use the names or initials of who's assigned to the feature (`feature/jd-settings`).
>
> * `"bug/<userstory/task number>-<problem>/"`: This example is helpful for immediately identifying bugs. An example of this technique could be `bug/1234-string-overflow`. Prefixing a branch with "bugfix" is also acceptable.

Once they are finished and everything's approved, each developer merges their changes into the `develop` branch.

Release Branches

Release branches are meant for last-minute polishing, minor bug fixes, and/or preparing for a new release of your software (how exciting!)

Let's examine how a release branch fits into our previous example. The following diagram shows what a release branch in GitFlow looks like:

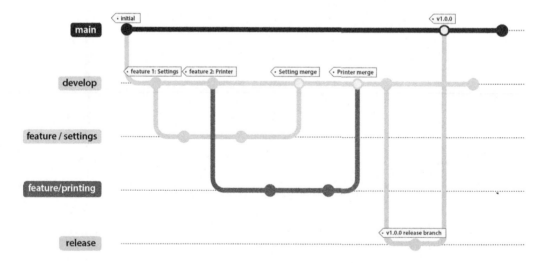

Figure 1.2: Release branch in GitFlow

Initially, developers create a feature branch based on what they were assigned. Once they merge their changes to `develop`, a new release is created from the `develop` branch. The release branch is merged into `main` and tagged with the version number. The main branch will now merge into the `develop` branch so developers have the latest changes in case there were code changes during the release process.

It's exactly the same as the feature branch, but if you notice, we're creating the `release` branch from the `develop` branch and not from the `main` branch.

After the `release` branch is created and confirmed to work as expected, the `release` branch is merged into the `main` branch.

Once merged into `main`, it's recommended to somehow identify a successful release. By convention, a tag with the version number is the best approach.

Hotfix branches

While most developers don't make coding mistakes (uh-huh), there are times when immediate changes are required to the `main` branch.

Going back to our example, it seems there was a problem with a developer's code. The application bombs when anyone selects the **Settings** option, making the application unusable. It requires a hotfix branch.

The following diagram shows an example of how to implement a hotfix branch:

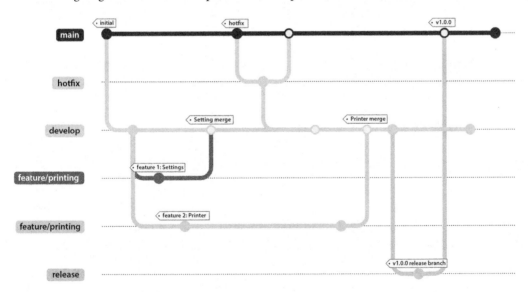

Figure 1.3: Hotfix branch in GitFlow

Hotfix branches are created from the `main` branch and, once the code is verified, need to be merged back into `main` and also the `develop` branch.

The long-running branches in GitFlow are main and develop. The short-lived branches include the features, hotfix, and bugfix branches.

Now that we've covered GitFlow and its branch types, we'll look at the next workflow, called GitHub Flow, and how it's different from GitFlow.

GitHub Flow

Over time, GitFlow has evolved into easier workflows. The first of these workflows was GitHub Flow, which was created in 2011.

GitHub Flow was meant to simplify things by removing the `develop` branch and creating features off the `main` branch.

The following diagram shows how feature branches work along with a hotfix branch.

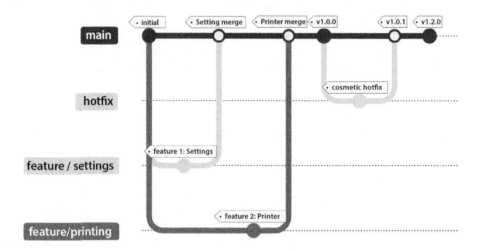

Figure 1.4: Hotfix branch in GitHub flow

In *Figure 1.4*, two features were created and both features were merged back into `main`. Immediately, version 1.0.0 was released. After the release of 1.0.0, some text was wrong on the site and the legal team requested for it to be fixed.

One of the developers created a hotfix branch, changed the label, requested a PR, got it approved, merged the change into `main`, updated the version, and immediately deployed the code to production.

What's the difference between a hotfix and a feature branch? A hotfix is a branch created from *main/ master*, with the code checked in, reviewed, updated, and immediately merged back into main/master. A feature branch is more of an organized or scheduled approach. The feature branch is created from the *develop branch*, with the code checked in, reviewed, and merged back into the feature branch. The feature branch is scheduled to be merged into a release branch.

So, where is the release branch? In each workflow, there is a release branch of some kind, which we'll review as follows. The concept of this branch is to always have a version error-free, tested, and ready to deploy at any time. Some small start-up companies use this type of workflow when starting out. With GitFlow considered as a baseline in the industry, it's easy to apply the GitFlow concepts when the team grows and is looking for a more structured workflow.

In GitHub flow, the long-running branch here is, again, main, where the short-lived branches are the features, hotfix, and bugfix branches.

After reviewing GitHub flow, let's move on to the last commonly used branching strategy, called GitLab Flow.

GitLab Flow

The final workflow that we'll cover is GitLab Flow. Created in 2014, GitLab Flow takes a different approach to the GitFlow workflow and combines feature branches with issue tracking using feature-driven development.

GitLab Flow takes release branches and turns them into stable environment branches, such as production and QA. Of course, you can create as many "environment branches" as necessary. If we had a QA environment branch, this may be used to test the final product. In *Figure 1.5*, we see the standard `feature` branches created from the `main` branch along with two other environment branches (pre-production and production).

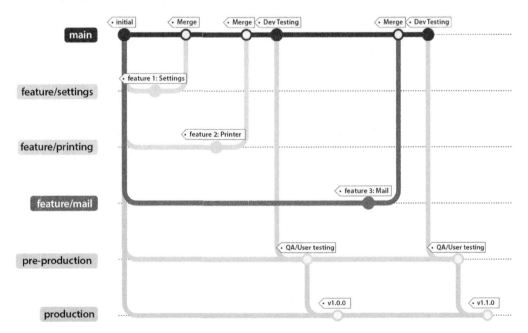

Figure 1.5: GitLab Flow

In GitLab Flow, main is considered a testing branch. Whether it's QA or a manager, it's a place to test the feature branches.

Similar to GitHub Flow, everything merges into the `main` branch. When the feature branch is committed, code reviews are conducted (these are mandatory), and merged to main, all tests (yes, *all*) run. If the tests run for longer than five minutes, configure them to run in parallel.

Once the testing is complete in main, `main` is pushed to `pre-production` for further testing and, finally, pushed to production. Since releases in GitLab Flow are based on tags, each tag should create a new release.

If a developer introduced a bug, it would have to be fixed in main first, then the environment branches second. The developer would have to create a bugfix branch, commit with a PR approval, conduct a code review, and merge the code along with running tests related to the bug before they could continue through the workflow.

Once tested in main, it's tagged and automatically promoted to pre-production and then production. Long-running branches in this workflow include main and the environment branches. Short-lived branches are the features, hotfix, and bugfix branches.

With each strategy we discussed in this section, we've seen how each one evolved from the initial GitFlow and (excuse the pun) branched into a better workflow.

The next sections refer to common etiquette when using source control.

Creating short-lived branches

Once you have initialized your repository and created your first branch, you can start writing code for your feature.

While this is exciting, this guideline is meant more for teams as opposed to an individual building a side project. The larger the team, the more critical this becomes to your workflow.

Let's look at an example using multiple feature branches in *Figure 1.6*.

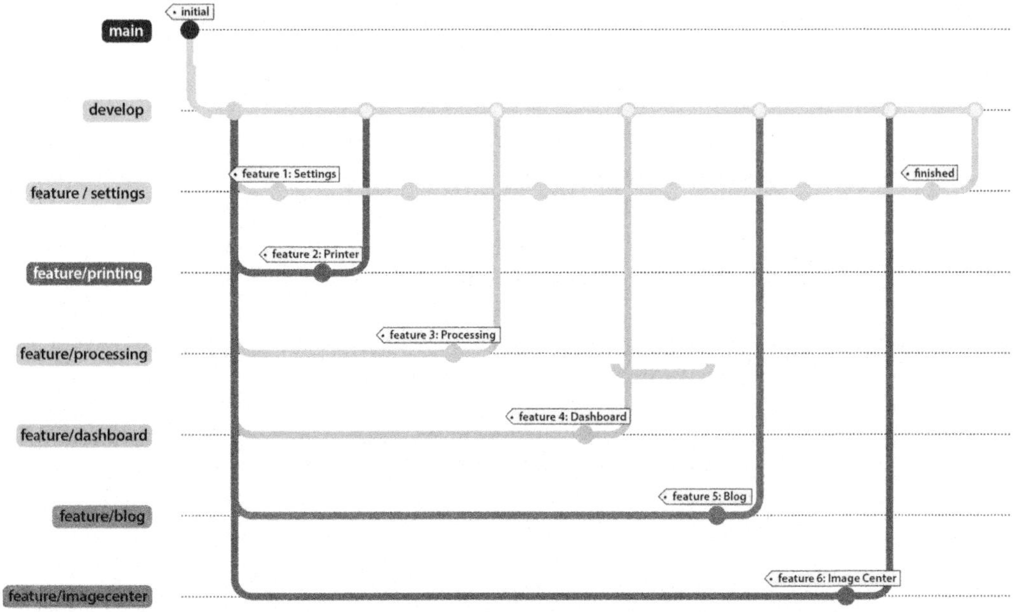

Figure 1.6: Long-lived feature branch (feature/settings)

Everyone is assigned their respective feature branches, which are created for them. As you can see, the developers are completing their features and checking them into develop.

However, the developer working on the settings feature (feature/settings) is behind. Their branch is becoming stale since they haven't updated their code over the week. It only contains their feature from when they first created their branch.

What do you think will happen if they decide to commit their code to the repository without updating their branch? There will be a lot of unhappy developers. Why?

The feature/settings branch will be committed and overwrite everyone who merged into the develop branch's changes. The shorter your branch's life expectancy, the less likely you'll experience merge conflicts.

It's best to perform updates on a daily basis, if not twice a day, to keep your branch from becoming stale.

Understanding Common Practices

Technically, knowing how to use source control is only half the battle. The other half is working as a team player while using source control. The ability to keep your fellow teammates in mind will take you further in your career as you become a considerate and trusted developer.

The following sections are meant as guidelines to help you succeed in working in a team environment. If you work as an individual developer on an open source project, it doesn't hurt to implement these practices as well.

Rebase when Private, Merge when Public

When working on a feature branch privately, there may be times where multiple commits are necessary. These commits add unnecessary noise to the `main/master` branch.

Rebasing your code takes a number of local commits and updates another branch with a single commit. It essentially rewrites the commit history. Of course, this differs from a merge. Merging is the process of taking all of the commits from one branch and merging the entire progress into another branch. Merging maintains the entire history of commits.

Think of rebasing as cleaning up your house before showing it to a potential buyer. If you make a number of mistakes in your local branch, you want your main/master branch to provide clear and concise comments as to what was applied to the code when committed.

Always "Get Latest" Before Committing

On the topic of keeping branches fresh, it's a good habit to "Get Latest" before you commit your code.

"Get Latest" pertains to you retrieving any updates from a central repository and applying updates to your local repository of code.

Whether you're using Git, **Team Foundation Server** (**TFS**), or another source control system, you need to keep your team in mind by always retrieving the latest code updates. Each source control tool has its own way of getting the latest version of the code. No matter what tool you use, it's always a good habit to get the latest version.

Since Git is considered the standard in the industry because of its flexibility and granular approach to source control, most development environments provide an interface (graphical or command line) out of the box for interacting with Git.

With Git, there are a couple of ways to push and pull changes:

- **Fetch**: Retrieves remote metadata to your local repository.
- **Pull**: Retrieves remote metadata *and* pulls a copy of those changes to the local repository.
- **Push**: Pushes commits to your remote branch.

- **Sync**: The process of performing a *pull* first, then a *push* second. Remember, get the latest changes and apply those changes to your own code, then push your committed changes to the server's repository.

Right before a commit, it's best to issue a pull to retrieve everything before committing your code.

Always Build and Test Before Committing

While this may seem like a simple concept after mentioning our previous guideline, there are a number of developers who continue to miss this step when committing code. Once you've pulled the latest, the next step is to compile the code and run your local unit tests against it. Don't assume the code you pulled is error-free.

It's a common circumstance that on a Friday afternoon, Developer B performs a pull to update their code, commits their code without compiling, and runs for the door.

What they didn't know is Developer-A committed code before Developer-B. It didn't compile and Developer-A already left for the weekend. Now Developer-B pulled the code and he was unable to compile it.

On Monday, they find out their code didn't build at all and the unit tests didn't pass.

Or worse, they receive a call on Friday night with this news.

Avoid Committing Binaries

Source control systems have been around for a while, and most are long in the tooth (SourceForge, anyone?), but all of them have been used as source code repositories.

Recently, there have been a number of **Content Management Systems** (**CMSes**) using source code systems as content repositories where they manage and version the assets of a website, such as images, MP3s, and videos.

However, in the case of developers, our content is our source code. Most developer repositories aren't even as big as a Word document.

If developers want to keep a "snapshot" of the system by committing everything, this defeats the purpose of source control.

For .NET applications, compiling an application means the `\bin` and `\obj` folders will contain assemblies. These assemblies are automatically created when compiled and *do not* need to be committed to a repository.

In most source control systems, an ignore file of some kind exists to filter and remove bloat from your repository before checking in your code. For example, in Git, there is a `.gitignore` file, which should include these `\bin` and `\obj` directories along with other file types not necessary for building your solution or project.

As a general guideline, when you clone a repository and immediately build it on a new machine, no errors should appear whether it's an internal corporate project or an open source framework on GitHub.

If committing assemblies to Git from either your own project or third-party projects is to keep it in a runnable state, you're doing it wrong. It's best not to commit any binaries into Git.

If you need a specific version of a third-party library, consider NuGet package management. When adding a NuGet package to your project, it automatically connects and retrieves the specific version and places it into the \bin folder, making the application compile, build, and successfully run every time.

Use tags for versioning

Tags are extremely helpful when using source control. As a matter of fact, they're what drives GitLab Flow. While tags are awesome for source control, they can be used for evil as well. For example, some companies use tags as comments throughout the entire workflow process, which is not recommended. Tags provide a way to place a flag in the ground to say, "This is version x.x.x." They're a marker of a code snapshot of a solid release. This signifies the code at this tag should build, compile, be tested, and run *with no changes made to the code and no errors.*

It's best to use tags strictly for versioning your releases throughout your workflow.

Summary

In this chapter, you learned about the different types of branching workflows available, including GitFlow, GitHub Flow, and GitLab Flow, and how each one works. Along with the workflows, you learned the industry-standard branch names, such as main/trunk/master, develop, features, release, and hotfix branches, and how they work in each workflow. You also learned the proper way to work with source control, such as always getting the latest code, when to rebase your code versus merging, allowing your branches to have a short lifespan, compiling and testing your code before committing, never checking in assemblies, and the proper use of tagging.

In the next chapter, we'll take the source code in our repository and create an automated build to create artifacts. We'll also cover how to automatically deploy it to a server.

2
CI/CD – Building Quality Software Automatically

In my career, someone once said to me, "*CI/CD is dead, long live CI/CD.*" Of course, this phrase doesn't mean it's completely dead. It simply means CI/CD is now becoming the standard for software development, a common practice developers should adopt and learn during a software development life cycle. It is now considered part of your development process as opposed to being a shiny, new process.

In this chapter, we'll review what **Continuous Integration/Continuous Deployment** (**CI/CD**) means and how to prepare your code for a pipeline. Once we've covered the necessary changes to include in your code, we'll discuss what a common pipeline looks like for building software. Once we understand the pipeline process, we'll look at two ways to recover from an unsuccessful deployment and how to deploy databases. We'll also cover the three different types of cloud services available to you (on and off-premises and hybrid) and review a list of the top CI/CD providers on the internet. Finally, we'll walk you through the process of creating a build for a sample application, along with other types of projects.

In this chapter, we will cover the following topics:

- What is CI/CD?
- Preparing your Code
- Understanding the Pipeline
- The Two "Falling" Approaches
- Deploying Databases
- The three Types of Build Providers
- CI/CD Providers
- Walkthrough of Azure Pipelines

After you've completed this chapter, you'll be able to identify flaws in software when you're preparing code for software deployment, understand what a common pipeline includes in producing quality software, identify two ways of recovering from an unsuccessful deployment, know how to deploy databases through a pipeline, understand the different types of CI/CD providers, and know some key players in the CI/CD provider space.

Finally, we'll walk through a common pipeline in Azure Pipelines to encompass everything we've learned in this chapter.

Technical requirements

For this chapter, the only technical requirements include having access to a laptop and an account for one of the cloud providers mentioned in the *CI/CD providers* section (preferably Microsoft's Azure Pipelines – don't worry, it's free).

Once you have reviewed how pipelines are created, you'll be able to apply the same concepts to other cloud providers and their pipeline strategies.

What is CI/CD?

In this section, we'll learn about what continuous integration and continuous deployment mean to developers.

Continuous Integration (**CI**) is the process of merging all developers' code into a mainline to trigger an automatic build process so that you can quickly identify issues with a code base using unit tests and code analysis.

When a developer checks their code into a branch, it's reviewed by peer developers. Once accepted, it's merged into a mainline and automatically starts a build process. This build process will be covered shortly.

Continuous Deployment (**CD**) is the process of consistently creating software to deploy it at any time.

Once everything has been built through the automated process, the build prepares the compiled code and creates artifacts. These artifacts are used for consistent deployments across various environments, such as development, staging, and production.

The benefits of implementing a CI/CD pipeline outweigh not having one:

- **Automated Testing**: When a commit is triggered, your tests are automatically executed along with your build. Think of this as someone always checking your code on commit.

- **Faster Feedback Loops**: As a developer, it's always great to receive immediate feedback to find out whether something works or not. If you receive an email where the build broke, you're on your own.

- **Consistent Builds**: Once you have a project being built on a build server, you can create builds on-demand – and consistently – with tests.

- **Collaboration Between Teams**: We're all in this together and CI/CD includes developers, system administrators, project managers/SCRUM masters, and QA testers, to name a few, to accomplish the goal of creating great software.

In this section, we reviewed the definition of what continuous integration and continuous deployment mean when developing software in an automated fashion and the benefits of implementing a CI/CD pipeline.

In the next section, we'll learn about certain code practices to avoid when automating software builds.

Preparing your Code

In this section, we'll cover certain aspects of your code and how they could impact the deployment of your software. Such software issues could include code not compiling (broken builds), avoiding relative path names, and making sure you wrote proper unit tests. These are a couple of the common errors I've experienced over the years; in this section, I'll also provide solutions on how to fix them.

Before we review a CI pipeline, there are a few caveats we should address beforehand. Even though we covered a lot in the previous chapter regarding version control, your code needs to be in a certain state to achieve "one-button" builds.

In the following sections, you'll learn how to prepare your code so that it's "CI/CD-ready" and examine the problems you could experience when deploying your software and how to avoid them.

Building Flawlessly

If a new person is hired and starts immediately, you want them to hit the ground running and begin developing software without delay. This means being able to point them to a repository and pull the code so that you can *immediately* run the code *with minimal setup*.

I say "minimal setup" because there may be permissions involved to gain access to certain resources in the company so that they can be run locally.

Nevertheless, the code should be in a runnable state, send you to a simple screen of some kind, and notify the user to follow up on a permissions issue or provide some notification to resolve the problem.

In the previous chapter, we mentioned how the code should compile at all times. This means the following:

- The code should always compile after a clone or checkout
- Unit tests should be included with the build, not in separate projects
- Your commit messages to version control should be meaningful (they may be used for Release Notes)

These standards allow your pipeline to fall into the pit of success. They help you create a build even faster and easier when your code is in a clean state.

Avoiding Relative Path Names with File-based Operations

One of the troublesome issues I've seen over the years when it comes to web applications is how files are accessed in a web application.

I've also seen file-based operations through a web page, where files were moved using relative paths and it went wrong. It involved deleting directories and it didn't end well.

For example, let's say you had a relative path to an image, as follows:

```
../images/myimage.jpg
```

Now, let's say you're sitting on a web page, such as `https://localhost/kitchen/chairs`.

If you went back one directory, you'd be in the kitchen with a missing image, not at the root of the website. According to your relative path, you're looking for an image directory at `https://localhost/kitchen/images/myimage.jpg`.

To make matters worse, if you're using custom routing, this may not even be the normal path, and who knows where it's looking for the image.

The best approach when preparing your code is to use a single slash (/) at the beginning of your URL since it's considered "absolute:"

```
/images/myimage.jpg
```

This makes it easier to navigate to the root when you're locating files on a website, regardless of what environment you're in. It doesn't matter if you are on `https://www.myfakewebsite.com/` or `http://localhost/`, the root is the root, and you'll always find your files when using a single slash at the beginning of your sources.

Confirming that your Unit Tests are Unit Tests

Tests in your code are created to provide checks and balances so that your code works as expected. Each test needs to be examined carefully to confirm it isn't doing anything out of the ordinary.

Unit tests are considered tests against code in memory, whereas integration tests are tests that require *ANY* external resources:

- Do your tests access any files? Integration test.
- Do you connect to a database to test something? Integration test.
- Are you testing business logic? Unit test.

As you're beginning to surmise, when you build your application on another machine, cloud services do not have access to your database server and also may not have the additional files you need for each test to pass.

If you are accessing external resources, it may be a better approach to refactor your tests into something a little more memory-driven. I'll explain why in *Chapter 7*, when we'll cover **unit testing**.

Creating Environment Settings

Whether you are in the middle of a project or are clicking **Create New Project…** for the first time, you need a way to create environment settings for your web application.

In ASP.NET Core applications, we are given `appsettings.json` and `appsettings.Development.json` configuration files out of the box. The `appsettings.json` file is meant to be a base configuration file and, depending on the environment, each `appsettings` file is applied and only existing properties are overwritten to the `appsettings.json` file.

One common example of this is connection strings and application paths. Depending on the environment, each file will have its own settings.

The environments need to be defined upfront as well. There will always be a development and release environment. There may be an option to create another environment called QA on another machine somewhere, so an `appsettings.qa.json` file would be required with its own environment-specific settings.

Confirm that these settings have been saved for each relevant environment since they are important in a CI/CD pipeline. *These environment settings should always be checked into version control with your solution/project* to assist the pipeline in deploying the right settings to the right environment.

In this section, we covered ways to prepare your code for a CI/CD pipeline by making sure we can build immediately after cloning or pulling the repository down locally, why we should avoid relative-based file paths, and confirmed we were using environment-specific application settings, making it easy to build and deploy our application.

With your code checked in, we can now move forward and describe all of the stages of a common pipeline.

Understanding the Pipeline

In this section, we'll cover the steps of what a common pipeline includes for building software when using a CI/CD service. When you reach the end of this section, you'll understand every step of the process in a common pipeline so that you can produce quality software.

A CI pipeline is a collection of steps required to code, build, test, and deploy software. Each step is not owned by a particular person but by a team working together and focusing on the goal to produce exceptional software. The good news is that if you followed the previous chapter's recommendations, you're already ahead of the game.

Each company's pipeline can vary from product to product, but there will always be a common set of steps for a CI process. It depends on how detailed your pipeline becomes based on your needs. The stages in the pipelines can be influenced by each stakeholder involved in the process. Of course, pulling code and building and testing are required for the developers, but a QA team requires the finished product (artifact) to be sent to another server for test purposes.

Figure 2.1 shows one common pipeline:

Figure 2.1 – One example of a build pipeline

As shown in *Figure 2.1*, the process is sequential when creating a software deployment. Here's a summary of the steps:

1. Pull code from a single repository.
2. Build the application.
3. Run unit tests/code analysis against the code that was built in *step 2*.
4. Create the artifacts.
5. Create a container (optional).
6. Deploy the artifact(s) to a server (development/QA/staging/production).

Now that we've defined a common pipeline, let's dig deeper into each step to learn what each process includes when you're building your software.

In the following subsections, we'll examine each process in detail based on the steps defined here.

Pulling Code

Before we build the application, we need to identify the project we're building in our pipeline. The pipeline service requires a repository location. Once you've provided the repository URL, the service can prepare the repository for compilation on their server.

In the previous section, we mentioned why your code needs to compile flawlessly after cloning. The code is cloned and built on a completely different machine from yours. If the application only works on your computer and no one else's, as the saying goes, "We'll have to ship your computer to all of our users." While this is a humorous saying in the industry, it's generally frowned upon when writing and deploying software in the real world.

Each of the DevOps services has its benefits. For example, Azure Pipelines can examine your repository and make assumptions based on the structure of your project.

After analyzing the project, it uses a file format called YAML (pronounced Ya-mel) to define how the project should be built. While YAML is now considered a standard in the industry, we won't deep-dive into everything YAML encompasses. YAML functionality could be a book on its own.

Azure takes your project's assumptions and creates a YAML template on how it should build your application.

It knows how to compile the application, identify whether a container is included in the project, and also retrieve NuGet packages before performing the build.

One last thing to mention is that most DevOp services allow one repository per project. The benefits of this approach include the following:

- **Simplicity**: It's simpler to manage and build one application as opposed to orchestrating hundreds of applications in a project.

- **Collaboration**: Instead of multiple teams focusing on one large project, it's easier to have one or two smaller teams working on a single, more manageable project.

- **Faster builds**: CI/CD pipelines are meant to provide fast feedback and even faster improvement. The smaller the project, the faster a build, test, and deployment will occur.

With that said, we are now ready to build the application.

Building the application

As mentioned previously, YAML files define how the service proceeds with building your application.

It's always a good practice to confirm the YAML file contains everything you need before building. If you have a simple project, the boilerplate included in the wizard may be all you need, but it allows you to make updates in case additional files are required, or other application checks.

It may take a couple of attempts to massage the YAML file, but once you get the file in a stable state, it's great to see everything work as expected.

Make sure you have retrieved all your code before building the application. If this step fails, the process kicks out of the pipeline.

If you checked in bad code and the build fails, the proper authorities (developers or administrators) will be notified based on the alert level and you'll be given the dunce hat or the stuffed monkey for breaking the build until someone else breaks it.

Next, we'll focus on running unit tests and other tests against the application.

Running Unit Tests/Code Analysis

Once the build is done, we can move forward with the unit tests and/or code analysis.

Unit tests should run against the compiled application. This includes unit tests and integration tests, but as we mentioned previously, be wary of integration tests. The pipeline services may not have access to certain resources, causing your tests to fail.

Unit tests, by nature, should be extremely fast. Why? Because you don't want to wait for 30 minutes for unit tests to run (which is painful). If you have unit tests taking that long, identify the longest-running unit tests and refactor them.

Once the code has been compiled and loaded, unit tests should be running every 10-30 seconds as a general guideline since they are memory-based.

While unit and integration tests are common in most testing scenarios, there are additional checks you can add to your pipeline, which include identifying security issues and code metrics to generate reports at the end of your build.

Next, our build creates artifacts to be used for deployments.

Creating Artifacts

Once the build succeeds and all of the tests pass, the next step is to create an artifact of our build and store it in a central location.

As a general rule, it's best to only create your binaries once. Once they've been built, they're available at a moment's notice. These artifacts can deploy a version to a server on a whim without going through the entire build process again.

The artifacts should be tamper-proof and never be modified by anyone. If there is an issue with the artifact, the pipeline should start from the beginning and create a new artifact.

Let's move on to containers.

Creating a Container

Once you have created the self-contained artifact, an *optional* step is to build a container around it or install the artifact in the container. While most enterprises use various platforms and environments, such as Linux or Windows, "containerizing" an application with a tool such as Docker allows it to run on any platform while isolating the application.

With containers considered a standard in the industry, it makes sense to create a container so that it can easily be deployed to any platform, such as Azure, **Amazon Web Services** (**AWS**), or Google Cloud Provider. Again, this is an optional step, but it's becoming an inevitable one in the industry.

When creating a new project with Visual Studio, you automatically get a container wrapper through a generated Docker file. This Dockerfile defines how the container will allow access to your application.

Once you've added the Dockerfile to your project, Azure identifies this as a container project and creates the container with the included project.

Lastly, we'll examine deploying the software.

Deploying the software

Once everything has been generated, all we need to do is deploy the software.

Remember the environment settings in your `appsettings.json` file? This is where they come in handy for deployments.

Based on your environment, you can assign a task to merge the appropriate environment JSON file into the `appsettings.json` file on deployment.

Once you have your environment settings in order, you can define the destinations of your deployments any way you like.

Deployments can range from FTP-ing or WebDeploy-ing the artifact or pushing the container to a server somewhere. All of these options are available out of the box.

However, you must deploy the same way to every environment. The only thing that changes is the `appsettings` file.

After a successful (or unsuccessful) deployment, a report or notification should be sent to everyone involved in the deployment's outcome.

In this section, we learned what a common pipeline includes and how each step relies on a successful previous step. If one step fails throughout the pipeline, the process immediately stops. This "conveyor belt" approach to software development provides repeatable steps, quality-driven software, and deployable software.

The Two "Falling" Approaches

In this section, we'll learn about two ways to recover from a failed software deployment. After finishing this section, you'll know how to use these two approaches to make a justified decision on recovering from a bad deployment.

In a standard pipeline, companies sometimes experience software glitches when deploying to a web server. Users may see an error message when they perform an action on the website.

What do you do when the software doesn't work as expected? How does this work in the DevOps pipeline?

Every time you build software, there's always a chance something could go wrong. You always need a backup plan *before* the software is deployed.

Let's cover the two types of recovery methods we can use when software deployments don't succeed.

Falling Backward (or fallback)

If various bugs were introduced into the product and the previous version doesn't appear to have these errors, it makes sense to revert the software or fall back to the previous version.

In a pipeline, the process at the end creates artifacts, which are self-contained, deployable versions of your product.

Here is an example of falling backward:

1. Your software deployment was a success last week and was marked as version 1.1 (v1.1).

2. Over 2 weeks, development created two new features for the software and wanted to release them as soon as possible.

3. A new build was created and released called version 1.3 (v1.3).

4. While users were using the latest version (v1.3), they experienced issues with one of the new features, causing the website to show errors.

5. Since the previous version (v1.1) doesn't have this issue and the impact is not severe, developers can redeploy v1.1 to the server so that users can continue to be productive again.

This type of release is called **falling backward**.

If you have to replace a current version (v1.3) with a previous version (v1.1) (except for databases, which I'll cover in a bit), you can easily identify and deploy the last-known artifact.

Falling Forward

If the fallback approach isn't a viable recovery strategy, the alternative is to fall forward.

When falling forward, the product team accepts the deployment with errors (warts and all) and continues to move forward with newer releases while placing a high priority on these errors and *acknowledging the errors will be fixed in the next or future release.*

Here is a similar example of falling forward:

1. Again, a software deployment was successful last week and was marked as version 1.5 (v1.5).

2. Over another 2 weeks, development created another new large feature for the software.

3. A new build was created and released called version 1.6 (v1.6).

4. While users were using the latest version (v1.6), they experienced issues with one of the new features, causing the website to show errors.

5. After analysis, the developers realized this was a "quick fix," created the proper unit tests to show it was fixed, pushed a new release through the pipeline, and immediately deployed the fixed code in a new release (v1.7).

This type of release is called **falling forward**.

The product team may have to examine each error and make a decision as to which recovery method is the best approach for the product's reputation.

For example, if product features such as business logic or user interface updates are the issue, the best recovery method may be to fall forward since the impact on the system is minimal and a user's workflow is not interrupted and productive.

However, if code *and* database updates are involved, the better approach would be to fall back – that is, restore the database and use a previous version of the artifact.

If it's a critical feature and reverting is not an option, a "hotfix" approach (as mentioned in the previous chapter) may be required to patch the software.

Again, it depends on the impact each issue has left on the system as to which recovery strategy is the best approach.

In this section, we learned about two ways to recover from unsuccessful software deployments: falling backward and falling forward. While neither option is a mandatory choice, each approach should be weighed heavily based on the error type, the recovery time of the fix, and the software's deployment schedule.

Deploying Databases

Deploying application code is one thing but deploying databases can be a daunting task if not done properly. There are two pain points when deploying databases: structure and records.

With a database's structure, you have the issue of adding, updating, and removing columns/fields from tables, along with updating the corresponding stored procedures, views, and other table-related functions to reflect the table updates.

With records, the process isn't as tricky as changing a table's structure. The frequency of updating records is not as regular, but when it does, happen that's when you either want to seed a database with default records or update those seed records with new values.

The following sections will cover some common practices when deploying databases in a CI/CD pipeline.

Backing up Before Deploying

Since company data is essential to a business, it's mandatory to back it up before making any modifications or updates to the database.

One recommendation is to make the entire database deploy a two-step process: back up the database, then apply the database updates.

The DevOps team can include a pre-deployment script to *automatically* back up the database before applying the database updates. If the backup was successful, you can continue deploying your changes to the database. If not, you can immediately stop the deployment and determine the cause of failure.

As discussed in the previous section, this is necessary for a "fallback" approach instead of a "fall forward" strategy.

Creating a Strategy for Table Structures

One strategy for updating a table is to take a non-destructive approach:

- **Adding a column**: When adding columns, place a default value on the column for when a record is created. This will prevent the application from erroring out when you add a record, notifying the user that a field didn't have a value or is required.

- **Updating/renaming a column**: Updating a column is a little different because you may be changing a data type or value in the database. If you're changing the column name and/or type to something else, add a new column with the new column type, make sure you default the value, and proceed to use it in your application code. Once the code is solid and is performing as expected, remove the old column from the table and then from your code.

- **Removing a column**: There are several different ways to handle this process. If the field was created with a default value, make the appropriate changes in your application code to stop using the column. When records are added to the table, the default value won't create an error. Once the application code has been updated, *rename* the column in the table instead of deleting it. If your code is still using it, you'll be able to identify the code issue and fix it. Once your code is running without error, it'll be safe to remove the column from your table.

While making the appropriate changes to table structures, don't forget about updating the additional database code to reflect the table changes, including stored procedures, views, and functions.

Creating a Database Project

If your Visual Studio solution connects to a database, there's another project type you need to add to your solution called the Database Project type. When you add this project to your solution, it takes a snapshot of your database and adds it to your project as code.

Why include this in your solution? There are three reasons to include it in your solution:

1. It provides a database schema as T-SQL when you create a database from scratch.

2. It allows you to version your database, in keeping with the **Infrastructure as Code (IaC)** paradigm.

3. When you're building your solution in Visual Studio, it automatically generates a DAC file from your Database Project for deployment with the option to attach a custom script. With the DAC included in your solution, the pipeline can deploy and update the database with the DAC file first. Once the database deployment (and backup) is finished, the pipeline can deploy the artifact.

As you can see, it's pretty handy to include with your solution.

Using Entity Framework Core's Migrations

Entity Framework has come a long way since its early days. Migrations are another way to include database changes through C# as opposed to T-SQL.

Upon creating a migration, Entity Framework Core takes a snapshot of the database and `DbContext` and creates the delta between the database schema and `DbContext` using C#.

With the initial migration, the entire C# code is generated with an `Up()` method.

Any subsequent migrations will contain an `Up()` method and a `Down()` method for upgrading and downgrading the database, respectively. This allows developers to save their database delta changes, along with their code changes.

Entity Framework Core's migrations are an alternative to using DACs and custom scripts. These migrations can perform database changes based on the C# code.

If you require seed records, then you can use Entity Framework Core's `.HasData()` method for easily creating seed records for tables.

In this section, we learned how to prepare our database deployment by always creating a backup, looked at a common strategy for adding, updating, and deleting table fields, and learned how to deploy databases in a CI/CD pipeline using either a DAC or Entity Framework Core's migrations.

The three Types of Build Providers

Now that we've learned how a standard pipeline works, in this section, we'll look at the different types of pipeline providers.

The three types of providers are on-premises, off-premises, and hybrid.

On-premises (meaning on-site or on-premises) relates to the software you own, which you can use to build your product at your company's location. An advantage of on-premises build services is that once you purchase the software, you own it; there isn't a subscription fee. So, if there's a problem with the build server, you can easily look at the software locally to identify and fix the problem.

Off-premises (or cloud) providers are the more common services used nowadays. Since everyone wants everything yesterday, it's quicker to set up and is usually an immediate way to create a software pipeline.

As you can guess, **hybrid services** are a mix of on-premises and off-premises services. Some companies like to keep control of certain aspects of software development and send the artifacts to a remote server for deployment purposes.

While hybrid services are an option, it makes more sense to use off-premises services for automated software builds.

In this section, we learned about three types of providers: on-premises, off-premises, and hybrid services. While these services are used in various companies, the majority of companies lean toward off-premises (or cloud) services to automate their software builds.

CI/CD Providers

In this section, we'll review a current list of providers on the internet to help you automate your builds. While there are other providers available, these are considered what developers use in the industry as a standard.

Since we are targeting ASP.NET Core, rest assured, each of these providers supports ASP.NET Core in its build processes and deployments.

Microsoft Azure Pipelines

Since Microsoft created ASP.NET Core, it only makes sense to mention its off-premises cloud offerings. It does offer on-premises and hybrid support as well. Azure Pipelines provides the most automated support for ASP.NET Core applications and deployment mechanisms to date.

While Azure is considered one of the biggest cloud providers in the world, I consider Azure Pipelines a small component under the Azure moniker.

> **Important note**
> You can learn more about Azure Pipelines here: `https://azure.microsoft.com/en-us/products/devops/pipelines/`.

GitHub Actions

When Microsoft purchased GitHub back in June of 2018, GitHub came out with an automation pipeline with GitHub Actions in October of the same year.

Since GitHub is a provider of all things source code-related, GitHub Actions was considered an inevitable step toward making code deployable.

After signing up to Actions, you'll notice the screens are very "Azure-ish" and provide a very similar interface when you're building software pipelines.

> **Important note**
>
> You can learn more about GitHub Actions here: `https://github.com/features/actions`.

Amazon CodePipeline

With Amazon commanding a large lead in the e-commerce landscape and with its Amazon Web Services (AWS offering), it also provides automated pipelines for developers.

Its pipelines are broken down into categories:

- `CodeCommit`: For identifying source code repositories
- `CodeArtifact`: A centralized location for build artifacts
- `CodeBuild`: A dedicated service for building your product based on updates in your repository, which are defined in `CodeCommit`
- `CodeDeploy`: For managing environments for deploying software
- `CodePipelne`: The glue that holds it all together

You can pick and choose the services you need based on your requirements. Amazon CodePipeline is similar to most cloud services, where you can use one service or all of them.

> **Important note**
>
> You can learn more about Amazon CodePipeline here: `https://aws.amazon.com/codepipeline/`.

Google CI

The final cloud provider is none other than Google CI. Google CI also provides the tools required to perform automated builds and deployments.

Google CI provides similar tools, such as Artifact Registry, source repositories, Cloud Build, and even private container registries.

As mentioned previously, once you understand how one cloud provider works, you'll start to see similar offerings in other cloud providers.

> **Important note**
>
> You can learn more about Google CI here: `https://cloud.google.com/solutions/continuous-integration`.

In this section, we examined four CI/CD cloud providers: Microsoft's Azure Pipelines, GitHub Actions, Amazon's CodePipeline, and Google's CI. Any one of these providers is a suitable candidate for creating an ASP.NET Core pipeline.

Walkthrough of Azure Pipelines

With everything we've discussed so far, this section will take us through a standard pipeline with a web application every developer should be familiar with: the ASP.NET Core web application.

If you have a web application of your own, you'll be able to follow along and make the modifications to your web application as well.

In this section, we'll demonstrate what a pipeline consists of by considering a sample application and walking through all of the components that will make it a successful build.

Preparing the Application

Before we move forward, we need to confirm whether the application in our version control is ready for a pipeline:

- Does the application compile and clone without errors?

- Do *all* the unit tests that accompany the application pass?

- Do you have the correct environment settings in your application? (For example, `appsettings.json`, `appsettings.qa.json`, and so on.)

- Will you deploy this application to a Docker container? If so, confirm you have a Dockerfile in the root of your application.

Again, the Dockerfile is optional, but most companies include one since they have numerous environments running on different operating systems. We'll include the Dockerfile in our web application to complete the walkthrough.

Once everything has been confirmed in our checklist, we can move forward and create our pipeline.

Introducing Azure Pipelines

Azure Pipelines is a free service for developers to use to automate, test, and deploy their software to any platform.

Since Azure is user-specific, you'll have to log in to your Azure Pipelines account or create a new one at `https://azure.microsoft.com/en-us/products/devops/pipelines/`. Don't worry – it's free to sign up and create pipelines:

1. To continue with this walkthrough, click on the **Start free with GitHub** button, as shown in *Figure 2.2*:

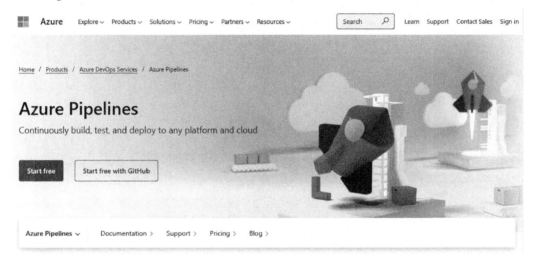

Figure 2.2 – The Azure Pipelines web page

Once you've logged in to Azure Pipelines, you are ready to create a project.

2. Click **New Project** in the top right-hand corner. Enter details for **Project Name** and **Description** and determine whether it's **Private** or **Public**.

3. Upon clicking **Create**, we need to define which repository to use in our pipeline.

Identifying the Repository

We haven't designated a repository for Azure Pipelines to use yet. So, we need to import an existing repository:

1. If you click on any option under **Files**, you'll notice a message saying <**YourProjectNameHere**> **is empty. Add some code!**. Sounds like solid advice.

2.   Click on the **Import** button under the **Import a repository** section, as shown in *Figure 2.3*:

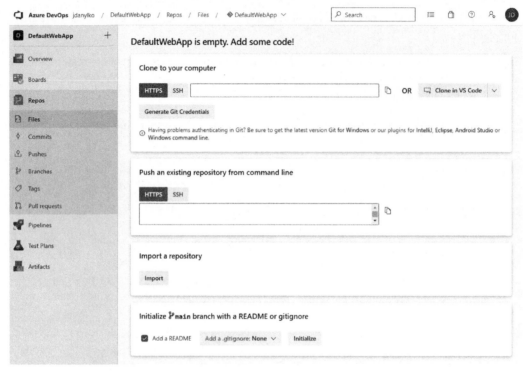

Figure 2.3 – Importing a repository

3.   Clicking on the **Import** button will result in a side panel popping out, asking where your source code is located. Currently, there is only Git and **Team Foundation Version Control** (**TFVC**).

4.   Since the code for DefaultWebApp is in Git, I copied the clone URL and pasted it into the text box, and then clicked the **Import** button at the bottom of the side panel, as shown in *Figure 2.4*:

Figure 2.4 – Identifying the repository Azure Pipelines will use

Azure Pipelines will proceed to import the repository. The next screen will be the standard **Explorer** view everyone is used to seeing, with a tree view on the left of your repository and a detailed list of files from the current directory on the right-hand side.

With that, we have finished importing the repository into Azure Pipelines.

Creating the Build

Now that we've imported our repository, Azure Pipelines makes this process extremely easy for us by adding a button called **Set up build**, as shown in *Figure 2.5*:

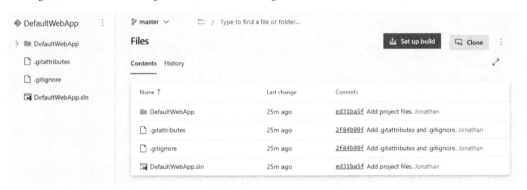

Figure 2.5 – Imported repository with a "Set up build" button as the next step

As vast as Azure Pipelines' features can be, there are several preset templates to use for your builds. Each template pertains to a particular project in the .NET ecosystem, along with not-so-common projects as well:

1. For our purposes, we'll select the **ASP.NET Core (.NET Framework)** option.

2. After the **Configure** step in our wizard (see the top?), we will come to the **Review** step, where we can examine the YAML file.

3. With that said, you aren't excluded from adding tasks at any time. There is **Show Assistant** to help you with adding new tasks to your existing YAML file.

For the DefaultWebApp example, we don't need to update our YAML file because we don't have any changes; this is because we want something very simple to create our build. The default YAML file looks like this:

```
# ASP.NET Core (.NET Framework)
# Build and test ASP.NET Core projects targeting the full .NET
Framework.
# Add steps that publish symbols, save build artifacts, and more:
```

```
# https://docs.microsoft.com/azure/devops/pipelines/languages/dotnet-
core

trigger:
- master

pool:
  vmImage: 'windows-latest'

variables:
  solution: '**/*.sln'
  buildPlatform: 'Any CPU'
  buildConfiguration: 'Release'

steps:
- task: NuGetToolInstaller@1

- task: NuGetCommand@2
  inputs:
    restoreSolution: '$(solution)'

- task: VSBuild@1
  inputs:
    solution: '$(solution)'
    msbuildArgs: '/p:DeployOnBuild=true /p:WebPublishMethod=Package
/p:PackageAsSingleFile=true /p:SkipInvalidConfigurations=true
/p:DesktopBuildPackageLocation="$(build.artifactStagingDirectory)\
WebApp.zip" /p:DeployIisAppPath="Default Web Site"'
    platform: '$(buildPlatform)'
    configuration: '$(buildConfiguration)'

- task: VSTest@2
  inputs:
    platform: '$(buildPlatform)'
    configuration: '$(buildConfiguration)'
```

This new file that Azure Pipelines created is called `azure-pipelines.yml`. So, where does this new `azure-pipelines.yml` file reside when it's created? It's committed to the root of your repository. Once we've confirmed everything looks good in the YAML file, we can click the **Save and run** button.

Once you've done this, a side panel will appear, asking you for a commit message and optional description, as well as to specify options on whether to commit directly to the master branch or create a new branch for this commit. Once you've clicked the **Save and run** button at the bottom of the side panel, it will commit your new YAML file to your repository and execute the pipeline immediately.

Creating the Artifacts

Once the build is running, you'll see something similar to *Figure 2.6*:

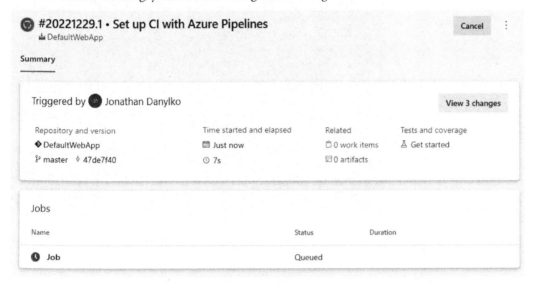

Figure 2.6 – Queueing up our DefaultWebApp build process

As shown at the bottom of the preceding screenshot, my job's status is **Queued**. Once it's out of the queue and executing, you can watch the builds progress by clicking on **Job** next to the blue clock at the bottom.

In terms of **DefaultWebApp**, this is what the build process looks as seen in *Figure 2.7*:

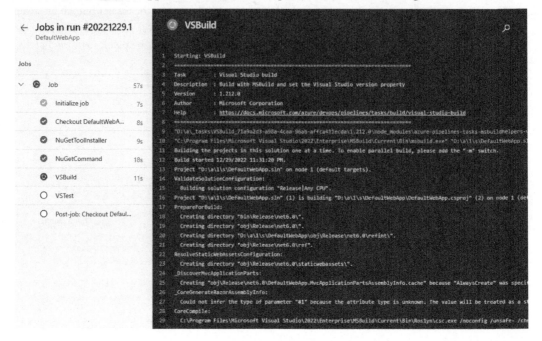

Figure 2.7 – The build progress of DefaultWebApp

Congratulations! You have created a successful pipeline and artifact.

For the sake of not writing an entire book on Azure Pipelines, next, we will move on to creating releases.

Creating a Release

With a completed and successful build, we can now focus on releasing our software. Follow these steps:

1. If you click on **Releases**, you'll see we need to create a new release pipeline. Click the **New Pipeline** button.

2. Immediately, you'll see a side panel appear with a list of templates you can choose from. Select **Empty job** at the top of the side panel, as shown in *Figure 2.8*:

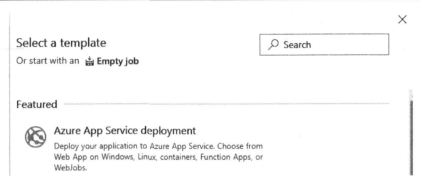

Figure 2.8 – Selecting an empty job template

There is a term in **Releases** called **Stages** where your software can go through several stages before it's sent to the final stage. These stages can also be synonymous with environments. These stages include development, QA, staging, and production. Once one stage has been approved (development), it moves to the next stage (QA) until the final one, which is usually production. However, these stages can get extremely complicated.

3. After you click the **Apply** button, you will see another side panel where you can define your stage. Since we are simply deploying the website, we'll call this the **Push to Site** stage.

4. After entering your **Stage** name (that just doesn't sound right), click the **X** button to close the side panel and examine the pipeline.

As shown in *Figure 2.9*, we need to add an artifact:

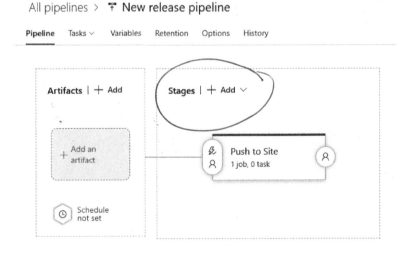

Figure 2.9 – The Push to Site stage is defined, but there's no artifact

5. When you click **Add an Artifact**, another side panel will slide open and ask you to add the artifact. Since we created an artifact in the previous subsection, we can populate all of our inputs with the **DefaultWebApp** project and source, as shown in *Figure 2.10*:

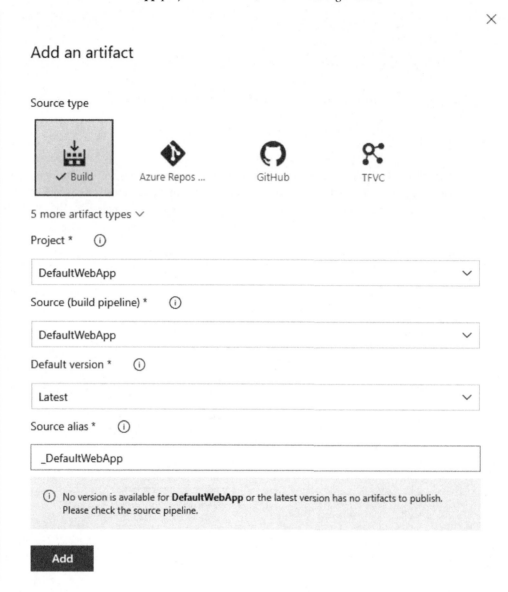

Figure 2.10 – Adding the DefaultWebApp artifact to our release pipeline

6. Click **Add** to add your artifact to the pipeline.

Deploying the Build

Once we have defined our stages, we can attach certain deployment conditions, both before and after, to each stage. The ability to define post-deployment approvals, gates, and auto-redeploy triggers is possible but disabled by default for each stage.

In any stage, you can add, edit, or remove any task you want by clicking on the "x job, x tasks" link under each stage's name, as shown in *Figure 2.11*:

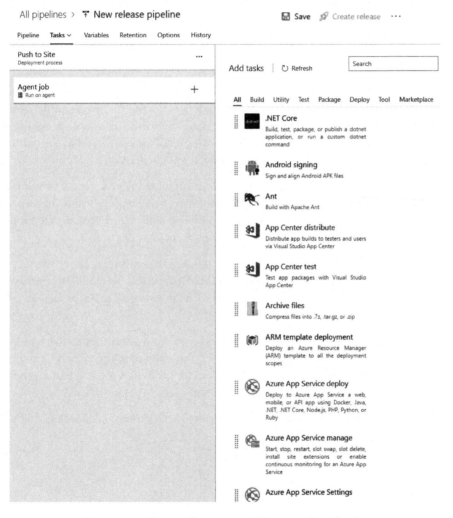

Figure 2.11 – Stages allow you to add any number of tasks

Each stage has an agent job, which can perform any number of tasks. The list of tasks to choose from is mind-numbing. If you can think of it, there is a task for it.

For example, we can deploy a website using Azure, IIS Web Deploy, or even simply a file that's been copied from one directory to another. Want to FTP the files over to a server? Click on the **Utility** tab and find **FTP Upload**.

Each task you add has parameters per topic and can easily be modified to suit a developer's requirements.

In this section, we covered how to create a pipeline by preparing the application to meet certain requirements. We did this by introducing Azure Pipelines by logging in and adding our sample project, identifying the repository we'll be using in our pipeline, and creating the build. Once we'd done this, we found our artifacts, created a release, and found a way to deploy the build.

Summary

In this chapter, we identified ways to prepare our code for a CI/CD pipeline so that we can build flawlessly, avoid relative path names with file-based operations, confirm our unit tests *are* unit tests, and create environment settings for our application. Once our code was ready, we examined what's included in a common CI/CD pipeline, including a way to pull the code, build it, run unit tests with optional code analysis, create artifacts, wrap our code in a container, and deploy an artifact.

We also covered two ways to recover from a failed deployment using a fall-back or fall-forward approach. Then, we discussed common ways to prepare for deploying a database, which includes backing up your data, creating a strategy for modifying tables, adding a database project to your Visual Studio solution, and using Entity Framework Core's migrations so that you can use C# to modify your tables.

We also reviewed the three types of CI/CD providers: on-premises, off-premises, and hybrid providers, with each one specific to a company's needs, and then examined four cloud providers who offer full pipeline services: Microsoft's DevOps Pipelines, GitHub Actions, Amazon's CodePipeline, and Google's CI.

Finally, we learned how to create a sample pipeline by preparing the application so that it meets certain requirements, logging in to Azure Pipelines and defining our sample project, identifying the repository we'll be using in our pipeline, and creating the build. Once the build was complete, it generated our artifacts, and we learned how to create a release and find a way to deploy the build.

In the next chapter, we'll learn about some of the best approaches for using middleware in ASP.NET Core.

3
Best Approaches for Middleware

Middleware is one of the most powerful concepts in ASP.NET Core. For legacy ASP.NET developers, *Middleware* is a relatively new term. Before middleware, there were HTTP handlers and modules, which required separate code to configure through a web.config. Middleware is now considered a first-class citizen in an ASP.NET application, making it easier to maintain in a single code base. First introduced in ASP.NET Core 1.0, the common request and response concepts are considered pipelines for your applications with the ability to control a request and response's body. This opens up a number of possibilities to create amazing features for your ASP.NET Core web applications.

At the beginning of this chapter, we'll examine how to use Middleware and some common built-in Middleware components found in almost every ASP.NET Core application. Next, we'll examine the three request delegates (Run, Map, and Use) and explain what each is used for in the pipeline. We'll also cover some ways to clean up your middleware and, finally, apply those concepts to building a simple middleware example.

In this chapter, we'll cover the following main topics:

- Using Middleware
- Common Practices for Middleware
- Creating an Emoji Middleware Component

By the end of this chapter, you'll have learned how Middleware works, how to use request delegates and standards when writing your own Middleware, and understand how to create your own Middleware components.

Technical requirements

Since this is the first chapter (one of many to come since we're in coding territory now) containing technical requirements, selecting your favorite editor that supports ASP.NET Core 7.0 or higher and C# code would be ideal. My top three editors are the following:

- Visual Studio (preferably 2022 or newer)

- Visual Studio Code

- JetBrains Rider

The editor we'll be using is Visual Studio 2022 Enterprise, but any version (Community or Professional) will work for this chapter.

The code for this chapter is located at Packt Publishing's GitHub repository located here: `https://github.com/PacktPublishing/ASP.NET-Core-8-Best-Practices`.

Using Middleware

Middleware is software you configure at the beginning of your application when the application starts. It's important to note that the Middleware you add should be based on your application's requirements. It's not necessary to add every single component. Streamlining your Middleware pipeline is important, which we'll discuss shortly.

 It's been said that the difference between a library and a framework is that a library is the code you call from your application, whereas a framework is structured a certain way to call your code. This is what Middleware has evolved into from earlier versions of ASP.NET.

In this section, we'll present the common flow of a Middleware pipeline and how to control what happens in a middleware component. By the end of this section, you'll understand how a middleware pipeline works.

Understanding the Middleware Pipeline

When your web application starts, Middleware is called and constructed once per *application lifetime*. Once the Middleware components are registered, they execute in a certain order. This order is important throughout the pipeline since each middleware component can rely on previously registered components.

For example, the Authentication component is important to configure before the Authorization component since we need to know who someone is before we can determine what they can do.

In *Figure 3.1*, we can see what a standard Middleware pipeline consists of in a web application, which we'll address next:

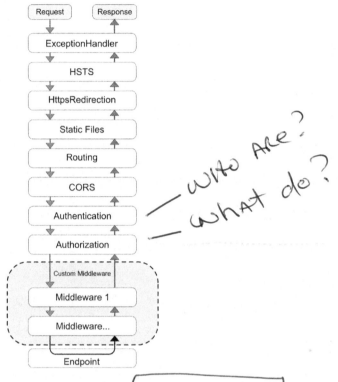

Figure 3.1 – Standard Middleware pipeline for an ASP.NET 8 Web Application

Each one of these components is optional, but some Middleware components are dependent on others. When a URL is requested by the user, the first Middleware component is hit. In this case, it's ExceptionHandler. Once ExceptionHandler is done, the pipeline moves on to the next component, which is the HSTS component. As we move through each Middleware component, we eventually reach the endpoint. Once the endpoint is processed, the response is sent back through the Middleware pipeline in reverse order.

As mentioned at the start of this section, your Middleware depends on what your application requires when adding additional components. If your application is a **Single-Page Application** (**SPA**), the inclusion of the CORS, Static Files, and Routing Middleware would be important.

Each middleware component is responsible for either passing information on to the next component in line based on your configuration or terminating the process. If they decide to terminate the pipeline, they are called *terminal Middleware* components. They purposefully stop the middleware from processing any other requests and exit the pipeline.

Using Request Delegates – Run, Use, and Map

With everything we've discussed so far, you're probably wondering how we create a pipeline.

The three request delegates available are the Run, Use, and Map extension methods. You've no doubt used them in your Program.cs code numerous times, but what's the difference between the three of them?

App →

Run

The Run() request delegate is strictly terminal middleware, meaning it will run and immediately quit the pipeline. It doesn't contain a next parameter. It simply runs and immediately terminates the pipeline.

If we look at the following code, this will immediately terminate the pipeline from executing:

```
app.Run(async context =>
{
    await context.Response.WriteAsync("This will terminate the web
        app.");
});
```

Notice there isn't a next parameter introduced in the delegate. The preceding code will write the message "This will terminate the web app." to the browser and immediately terminate the pipeline.

Services → App →

Use

The Use() request delegate is used to chain multiple request delegates together in the pipeline.

The key to implementing a proper Use request delegate is the use of await next.Invoke(). next.Invoke() will execute the next middleware component in sequential order. Anything before this line will be processed on the request, and anything after this line will be processed on the response back to the user.

Let's look at a code sample of two anonymous Middleware components in the following code snippet:

```
app.Use(async (context, next) =>
{
    await context.Response.WriteAsync("In the first middleware call.\
        r\n");

    await context.Response.WriteAsync("Executing the next
        Middleware...\r\n");
    await next();

    await context.Response.WriteAsync("In the first middleware call...on
```

```
the return trip.\r\n");
});

app.Use(async (context, next) =>
{
    await context.Response.WriteAsync("We're in the second middleware
        call\r\n");

    await next();

    await context.Response.WriteAsync("On our way back from the second
        middleware call\r\n");
});
```

This code creates the following output:

```
In the first middleware call.
Executing the next Middleware...
We're in the second middleware call
On our way back from the second middleware call
In the first middleware call...on the return trip.
```

You'll notice anything before the next.invoke() line of code is executed and then the execution moves on to the next Middleware in the order. Once we get to the end of the Middleware pipeline, we make the return trip back, which executes all of the code *after* each Middleware's await next(); statement.

After each Middleware component is executed, the application runs and then returns in reverse order.

Map

The Map() request delegate is meant for branching the pipeline based on a certain request path or route. While this is for specific Middleware conditions, creating a new map is highly unlikely. It's usually best to use pre-built Middleware components such as .MapRazorPages(), .MapControllers(), or any of the other .MapXxxx() methods. These methods already have pre-defined routes in place. Most routing occurs inside other extensions like the previously mentioned Middleware methods.

There is also a MapWhen() extension method for conditional middleware branching based on the result of a given predicate. For example, if you want to create a controlled maintenance page for your site, you could use a simple Boolean called underMaintenance and use it to display a simple message until your site is available again:

```
app.MapWhen(_ => underMaintenance, ctx =>
    ctx.Run(async context =>
    {
        await context.Response
```

```
                .WriteAsync("We are currently under maintenance.");
        })
   );
```

In the preceding code, we add our `.MapWhen()` delegate to use a specific Boolean to identify whether we are under maintenance or not. Notice we're using the `.Run` delegate because we don't want to continue any further down the Middleware pipeline. This approach is just one example of Middleware's flexibility.

> **Using Built-in Middleware Components**
>
> While you can create your own Middleware components, the best approach is to see whether a Middleware component exists from the large number of built-in components already available to you. The entire list is located at `https://learn.microsoft.com/en-us/aspnet/core/fundamentals/middleware/?view=aspnetcore-7.0#built-in-middleware`. This chart provides a description of each Middleware component and the location of where to place it in the Middleware pipeline. In addition to the built-in components, use NuGet to find innovative Middleware components as well.

In this section, we covered the middleware pipeline, learned how to use the request delegates and what each request delegate can do, and learned about all of the built-in middleware components available for ASP.NET web applications. In the next section, we'll examine the common practices for using Middleware.

Common Practices for Middleware

In this section, we'll review a number of common practices when writing your own middleware to keep everything running optimally in your web application. Let's get started!

Defer to Asynchronous

When working with Middleware, we want to get the best performance possible so our users can begin working in the application. As more users continue to use the application, performance may suffer.

A synchronous operation is where code is executed and the application has to wait for it to finish, meaning it's single-threaded and runs on the application's main thread, but when an asynchronous operation is executed, it creates a new thread and lets the framework know what to call when it's finished processing. This is signified through the `async/await` keywords.

For the majority of Middleware operations, it's best to use asynchronous calls when applicable. This will increase Middleware (and application) performance along with better scalability and responsiveness.

Prioritizing the Order

One of the more important points of setting up your Middleware is to confirm everything is in the right order.

Compare your application's requirements with the previous chart to identify what middleware components you need and what their correct order is for your web application.

For example, if you want to include a W3C Logging Middleware component (which is included in the built-in Middleware components from Microsoft), it has to be at the beginning of the pipeline to log any subsequent requests made throughout the application. Each component has its place in the pipeline.

Consolidating existing Middleware

When you create a new ASP.NET project, you'll notice the collection of app.UseXxx() listed in Program.cs. While this is the "out-of-the-box" approach for preparing your pipeline, there are other ways to organize and register components for your application.

One approach is to use extension methods based on how you logically partition your uses into similar groupings while keeping the components in the same order.

One example would be to move all client Middleware into its own extension method called .UseClientOptions():

```
public static class WebApplicationExtensions
{
    public static void UseClientOptions(this WebApplication app)
    {
        app.UseHttpsRedirection();
        app.UseStaticFiles();
    }
}
```

Now, the code in your Program.cs file contains one line, and you know exactly what the extension method does:

```
app.UseClientOptions();
```

When using this approach, your Program.cs file is cleaner, well maintained, and contains fewer lines of code.

Other possible areas to partition are as follows:

- UseDataXxxxx() – Centralized location for connection strings for your application
- UseMapping()/UseRouting() – Create a collection of routes for your application and APIs

- `RegisterDependencyInjection()` – Centralize the classes in a number of extension methods similar to this grouping approach, but partitioned by sections in your application – for example, `RegisterDIPayroll()` for registering classes pertaining to the Payroll section of the application

While these are merely suggestions, the concept is to trim the size of the `Program.cs` file so other developers understand the approach with fewer lines of code, and it provides enough clarity for other developers to extend the technique further.

As a recommendation, include all of the important Middleware components upfront and confirm the application runs as expected, *then* perform your refactoring by creating your groups for consolidation. Remember, the order of Middleware components matters.

Encapsulating your Middleware

When creating your first middleware component, you may be tempted to create it and use it in this fashion:

```
app.Use(async (context, next) =>
{
    app.Logger.LogInformation("In our custom Middleware...");

    // Prepare work for when we write to the Response
    await next();
    // work that happens when we DO write to the response.
});
```

One problem with this approach is the preceding code can make your `Program.cs` file look a little messy if you have a large number of custom middleware components.

Once you have your custom component working, it's better to encapsulate it into its own class for increased reusability. If we use our previous example, our new class would look like this:

```
public class MyFirstMiddleware
{
    private readonly ILogger _logger;
    private readonly RequestDelegate _next;

    public MyFirstMiddleware(ILogger logger, RequestDelegate next)
    {
        _logger = logger;
        _next = next;
    }
}
```

```
    public async Task InvokeAsync(HttpContext context)
    {
        _logger.LogInformation("In our custom Middleware...");

        // Prepare work for when we write to the Response
        await _next(context);
        // work that happens when we DO write to the response.
    }
}
```

In this example, the `MyFirstMiddleware` component is a simple class that can contain only one method of `Invoke` or `InvokeAsync`. As mentioned before, we'll use the `InvokeAsync` asynchronous method.

If you're wondering how `ILogger` is passed in, ASP.NET Core has a number of classes automatically registered with its out-of-the-box dependency injection library. `ILogger` is one of those classes, so we don't need to worry about passing it through to our `MyFirstMiddleware` component.

We can use our class in our `Program.cs` file like this:

```
app.UseMiddleware<MyFirstMiddleware>();
```

However, since we're good ASP.NET developers, we can definitely improve the code. Most middleware components have extension methods attached to them to make them easier to use (which we'll add now with the following code):

```
public static class MyFirstMiddlewareExtensions
{
    public static IApplicationBuilder UseMyFirstMiddleware(
        this IApplicationBuilder builder)
    {
        return builder.UseMiddleware<MyFirstMiddleware>();
    }
}
```

Our `Program.cs` file is much simpler and cleaner now:

```
app.UseMyFirstMiddleware();
```

These simple practices make a developer's life easier for reusability and encapsulation.

In this section, we covered a number of standard methods for writing maintainable and efficient Middleware by using asynchronous calls, prioritizing the order of your components, and consolidating the existing Middleware into extension methods. We also examined how to encapsulate components by creating classes and extension methods to make the code easier to read.

Creating an Emoji Middleware Component

With the rise of emoticons…sorry, emojis…in the 2000s, a number of legacy websites use the old-style of text-based emoticons instead of the more modern emojis. Legacy **Content Management Systems (CMSs)** must have a lot of these text-based characters in their content. To update a website's content to replace all of these emoticons with proper emojis sounds extremely time-consuming.

In this section, we'll apply our standards in creating an emoji Middleware component where, if it detects a text-based emoticon, it'll convert it to a more modern emoji.

Encapsulating the Middleware

With this new Middleware component, we want to create it in its own class in `EmojiMiddleware.cs`.

Here is the first draft of our component:

```
public class EmojiMiddleware
{
    private readonly ILogger _logger;
    private readonly RequestDelegate _next;

    public EmojiMiddleware(ILogger logger, RequestDelegate next)
    {
        _logger = logger;
        _next = next;
    }

    public async Task InvokeAsync(HttpContext context)
    {
        await _next(context);
    }
}

public static class EmojiMiddlewareExtensions
{
    public static IApplicationBuilder UseEmojiMiddleware(
        this IApplicationBuilder builder)
    {
        return builder.UseMiddleware<EmojiMiddleware>();
    }
}
```

While this isn't very exciting, this boilerplate meets all of the previously-mentioned standards for building Middleware components, which include the following:

- An encapsulated Middleware component
- Using Asynchronous methods (`InvokeAsync()`)
- An extension method for reuse and readability

We can now focus on the conversion process.

Examining the Component's Pipeline

[handwritten: Pipeline Faster than Stream / 2 ways process Request/Response / Stream vs Pipeline]

In Middleware, there are two ways to process a request and response: by using either streams or pipelines. While pipelines are the better option for high performance, we'll focus on streams for our `EmojiMiddleware`. We'll examine pipelines in a later chapter.

Our middleware stream is located in `HttpContext` through `HttpRequest.Body` and `HttpResponse.Body`. In our `Invoke` method, we conveniently pass in an `HttpContext`.

Our first order of business is to create the `EmojiStream`. This will accept a simple response stream and read it into memory. Once we have our HTML, we can search and replace our emoticons. We need a map to identify the text-based characters and what image to replace them in our HTML.

To make our life a little easier, we'll inherit from the `Stream` base class and simply override specific methods to fit our needs. The only implementation our `EmojiStream` class needs is our text-based emoticons-to-emojis mapping and the `.Write()` method, as shown with the following code:

```
public class EmojiStream: Stream
{
    private readonly Stream _responseStream;
    private readonly Dictionary<string, string> _map = new()
    {
        { ":-)", " :) " },
        { ":)", " :) " },
        { ";-)", " ;) " }
    };

    public EmojiStream(Stream responseStream)
    {
        ArgumentNullException.ThrowIfNull(responseStream);

        _responseStream = responseStream;
    }
```

```csharp
public override bool CanRead => _responseStream.CanRead;
public override bool CanSeek => _responseStream.CanSeek;
public override bool CanWrite => _responseStream.CanWrite;
public override long Length => _responseStream.Length;
public override long Position
{
    get => _responseStream.Position;
    set => _responseStream.Position = value;
}

public override void Flush()
{
    _responseStream.Flush();
}

public override int Read(byte[] buffer, int offset, int count)
{
    return _responseStream.Read(buffer, offset, count);
}

public override long Seek(long offset, SeekOrigin origin)
{
    return _responseStream.Seek(offset, origin);
}

public override void SetLength(long value)
{
    _responseStream.SetLength(value);
}

public override void Write(byte[] buffer, int offset, int count)
{
    var html = Encoding.UTF8.GetString(buffer, offset, count);
    foreach (var emoticon in _map)
    {
        if (!html.Contains(emoticon.Key)) continue;

        html = html.Replace(emoticon.Key, emoticon.Value);
    }
    buffer = Encoding.UTF8.GetBytes(html);

    _responseStream.WriteAsync(buffer, 0, buffer.Length);
}
}
```

At the beginning of the code, we create our map of emoticons to look for in the HTML. The `EmojiStream` class is fairly common, except for the `WriteAsync()` method. We'll grab the HTML using the `GetString()` method and search for each emoticon in the response. If we find one, we'll replace it with an image tag and, finally, write the bytes back into the stream.

Since we're focused on using streams in the Middleware, we'll pass a stream into the constructor instead of creating a new instance.

With the middleware piece left, we can use the `EmojiStream` in our class:

```
public class EmojiMiddleware
{
    private readonly RequestDelegate _next;

    public EmojiMiddleware(RequestDelegate next)
    {
        _next = next;
    }

    public async Task InvokeAsync(HttpContext context)
    {
        using var buffer = new MemoryStream();

        // Replace the context response with our buffer
        var stream = context.Response.Body;
        context.Response.Body = buffer;

        // Invoke the rest of the pipeline
        // if there are any other middleware components
        await _next(context);

        // Reset and read out the contents
        buffer.Seek(0, SeekOrigin.Begin);

        // Adjust the response stream to include our images.
        var emojiStream = new EmojiStream(stream);

        // Reset the stream again
        buffer.Seek(0, SeekOrigin.Begin);

        // Copy our content to the original stream and put it back
        await buffer.CopyToAsync(emojiStream);
        context.Response.Body = emojiStream;
    }
}
```

While our Middleware component takes a simple `RequestDelegate`, the majority of the component is in the `InvokeAsync()` method. First, we create a new stream for our response. Next, we replace the standard response with our own stream. When we are coming back from our endpoint, we create our `EmojiStream` instance and pass in our custom stream to the `Response.Body`.

Since `HttpContext` exposes `HttpRequest.Body` and `HttpResponse.Body` as streams, it's easier to pass `HttpContext` into custom middleware components.

Of course, we can't forget our extension method, which is shown here:

```
public static class EmojiMiddlewareExtensions
{
    public static IApplicationBuilder UseEmojiMiddleware(
        this IApplicationBuilder builder)
    {
        return builder.UseMiddleware<EmojiMiddleware>();
    }
}
```

This extension method is considered a façade to hide the details of what our `EmojiStream` is doing behind the scenes. While we could use the `builder.UseMiddleware<EmojiMiddleware>()` syntax in our `Program.cs` file, the extension method cleans it up a bit, giving it a professional look.

The last thing required is to add the `EmojiMiddleware` to the pipeline in your `Program.cs` file:

```
app.UseEmojiMiddleware();
```

After creating a brand new ASP.NET Core website, we'll add the following HTML to the bottom of our Index page:

```
<div class="text-center">
    <h2>Smile, you're on candid camera. :-) :)</h2>
    <p>It even works inside ;-) a paragraph.</p>
</div>
```

When we run the application without our middleware component, we have the following output (*Figure 3.2*):

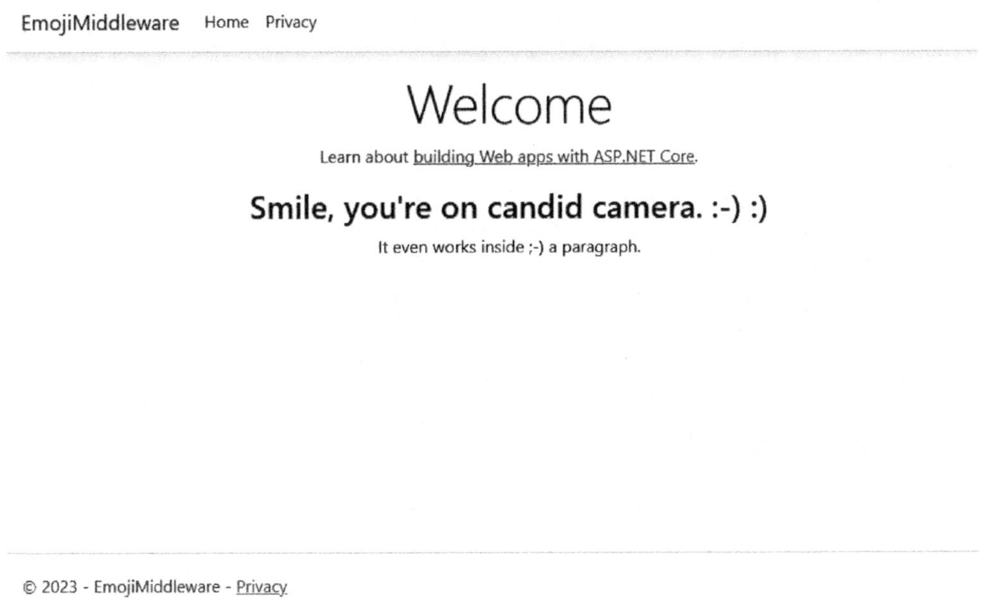

EmojiMiddleware　　Home　Privacy

Welcome

Learn about <u>building Web apps with ASP.NET Core</u>.

Smile, you're on candid camera. :-) :)

It even works inside ;-) a paragraph.

© 2023 - EmojiMiddleware - <u>Privacy</u>

Figure 3.2 – Before our EmojiMiddleware is added to the pipeline

When we add our Emoji Middleware to our pipeline and run our application again, we receive the following output (*Figure 3.3*):

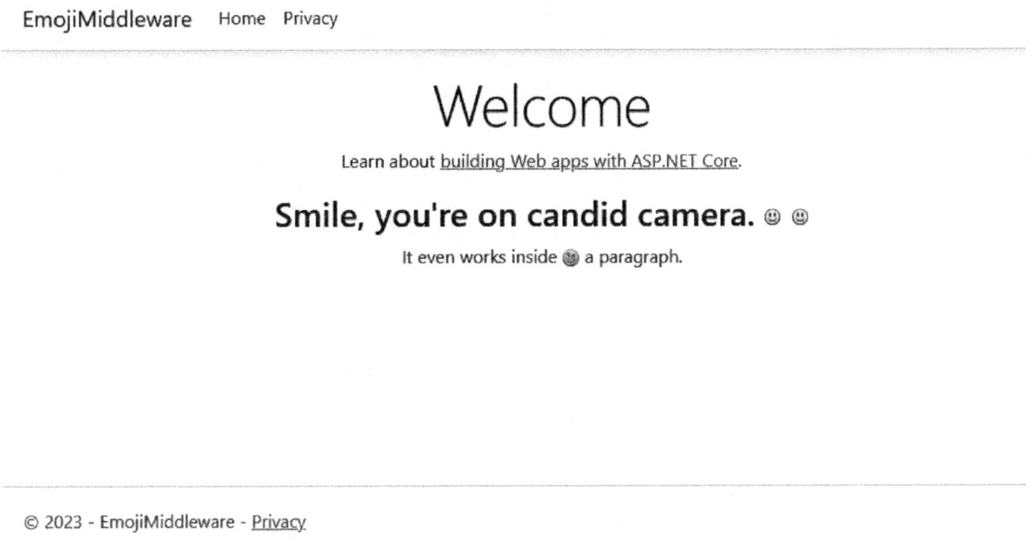

EmojiMiddleware　　Home　Privacy

Welcome

Learn about <u>building Web apps with ASP.NET Core</u>.

Smile, you're on candid camera. ☺ ☺

It even works inside ☺ a paragraph.

© 2023 - EmojiMiddleware - <u>Privacy</u>

Figure 3.3 – After our EmojiMiddleware is added to the pipeline

In this section, we built our first Middleware component by encapsulating the logic in a class, examined the components pipeline using streams, and used the Middleware component in a web application.

Summary

In this chapter, we have gained a solid understanding of the Middleware pipeline, its components, and best practices for using Middleware in ASP.NET Core. We also learned about common practices when using Middleware, such as always using asynchronous methods, prioritizing the order, consolidating your Middleware components into groups, and encapsulating your Middleware into classes. Knowing these Middleware concepts is key to creating maintainable and readable code.

Finally, we finished the chapter by creating a simple component to replace text with an image in a stream for the user.

In the next chapter, we'll begin looking at applying security to new and existing applications.

4

Applying Security from the Start

Next to performance, security should always be a top priority when building web applications. The ability to create secure web applications continues to be a problem with the evolving landscape of internet threats such as **cross-site scripting** (**XSS**) and injection techniques. While the best developer can safeguard an application against even the worst threat, most attacks succeed through human interaction and environmental issues. The best approach for developers to protect their applications is to start from the ground up and create as many roadblocks as possible to deter even the most vigilant attackers from gaining access to their systems.

First, we'll learn how to identify highly sensitive data and how to secure access. We'll then move on to common security practices and provide various ASP.NET Core features that you can apply to your applications. Finally, we'll review the top three security threats according to the **Open Worldwide Application Security Project** (**OWASP**) and how to safeguard your application.

In this chapter, we're going to cover the following main topics:

- Developing Security
- Common Security Practices
- Safeguarding Against the Top 3 Security Threats

By the end of this chapter, you'll understand what is considered sensitive data, a variety of common security practices in the industry, and how to safeguard yourself against the top three threats according to the OWASP Foundation.

Technical requirements

While we will talk about security in this chapter, most of the discussion will contain small snippets of code that you can include in your projects. Access to a code editor isn't necessary for this chapter to understand the essentials of security at a developer level.

The code files for this chapter can be found here: `https://github.com/PacktPublishing/ASP.NET-Core-8-Best-Practices`.

Developing Security

In this section, we'll examine terms and concepts regarding how to identify the data you need to secure and explain three extremely important ways to secure your website.

Too often, when developers start to build an ASP.NET web project, security is usually applied at the end of a project as opposed to being proactive and aware of security measures. One approach for implementing security is to examine your applications and look for these types of highly sensitive data throughout:

- Name and location
- Usernames and passwords
- Contact information (phone number, email address, and so on)
- Social security number
- Financials (customer plans, credit cards, and so on)
- Database connections
- Custom settings

Depending on the intent of the web application, other types might be involved, such as specific access to a section where permissions are implied. Other types of data could be considered sensitive based on industry or even government regulations.

Security in your application should be examined based on the criteria discussed in the following sections.

Do I have any sensitive data to protect?

Based on your application and the list in the previous section, ask yourself, "If any of the data is leaked and made public, would there be a problem?"

Exposing any data from the aforementioned sources would be a disaster. Keep sensitive information contained using encryption, access controls, and secure coding practices, and use it only when necessary.

Am I exposing anything through the application?

When moving from one web page to another, am I passing something sensitive when maneuvering through the site? Is the application using primary keys in the URL? How is data passed to the next page?

Be mindful of visible clues to the users that contain information such as primary keys or sensitive information. We'll discuss this later in this chapter.

Am I sanitizing user input?

When requesting input from a user, it's always a good practice to sanitize the data. Sanitization, or scrubbing, is the process of taking user input and confirming it's not malicious content that could compromise the system. One philosophy is to never trust submitted data.

It's extremely important to use light validation with JavaScript/HTML on the client side, along with heavy validation and sanitization of data on the server.

Light validation would include ensuring the required fields are populated and contain the minimum and maximum length of data, and that certain fields meet a particular format (such as phone numbers, credit cards, and so on).

Heavier validation would reaffirm the light validation but also confirm various scenarios, such as that a user has access to something, referenced entities exist, or data disguised to cause malicious activity.

Securing Access

When building a website, it's best to think about whether a user is required to log in to your site or not. If you're creating a blog, there wouldn't be a need to have users log in to view a post. They would just view it anonymously.

However, if you require a user to log in to your website, there is a minimum of three mandatory requirements you must understand to *begin* to secure your application. We'll look at them in the following sections.

Authentication

When authenticating a user, you are *identifying and validating who they are* when they log in to your system.

This is the primary concept of Microsoft's Identity framework. It offers various methods to authenticate a user using either username/password, the ability to use third-party social networks (such as Facebook, Google, or Twitter), use **two-factor authentication** (**2FA**), or even use third-party authenticators.

You may have already experienced this on a website where you have to enter your username and password. That is step one in authenticating a user. Once verified, you are then asked to enter the code that's been sent to your email or the authenticator app on your phone. That is step two.

Many websites use a username and password to log in. While this is the bare minimum to secure a website, it may help to implement additional security measures when authenticating a user.

Again, it's a better approach to create as many additional roadblocks to protect your application from attackers as possible. The more obstacles, the less likely your site will be compromised.

Authorization

Once the user has authenticated, what can they do in the system? This is where authorization enters the picture.

Authorization is the *process of granting permission to do something in a system or on a website*. For example, authors of a blog are permitted to update their articles when they log in, but they are not allowed to edit other articles unless they are authorized to do so by an administrator. An authorization system would need to be in place for this to work.

As mentioned in the *Authentication* section, Microsoft's Identity framework contains various techniques for implementing role-based and user-based claims throughout the system. In our previous example, we mentioned that authors are only allowed to update their own articles. In a role-based system, the authors could be grouped into an "Authors" role, allowing them to create and update their own articles. In a user-based system, special privileges could be assigned at the user level, such as editing other authors' articles.

While Microsoft Identity is flexible enough to incorporate any kind of authorization mechanism, developers should think about how to structure application-level authorizations from the very beginning before writing one line of code.

Authorizations are extremely important when you're identifying what a logged-in user can (and can't) do on your website.

Secure Sockets Layer (SSL)

If you're building a website, SSL is *absolutely required*.

The necessity to have an SSL-enabled website protects you for the following reasons:

- You want your visitors to know they are on a secure website.

- It prevents others on the same network viewing your login credentials.

- HTTPS helps prevent a **Man-in-the-Middle** (**MITM**) attack, where an attacker inserts themselves into a conversation between two users, possibly altering the exchange of data.

- **Search Engine Optimization** (**SEO**). Google and other search engines use HTTPS as a ranking signal (reference: `https://developers.google.com/search/blog/2014/08/https-as-ranking-signal`). If you wanted to increase your chances of reaching number one in the search results, you should make your site SSL-enabled.

Most hosting companies *include* an SSL certificate free of charge for your sites. That's how important SSL is to a website.

In this section, we identified what is considered sensitive data and learned about how to secure access using three critical concepts when building an ASP.NET Core application.

In the next section, we'll look over some common security practices you can immediately start using in your applications.

Common Security Practices

As a developer, security seems to be a black box sometimes. You always hear about incidents where websites have been hacked, but you might think to yourself, "That couldn't happen to me," until it happens to you. When you witness a website you built being attacked first-hand, it's a humbling experience.

While the techniques we're about to cover only scratch the surface for ASP.NET websites, they encourage developers to become more proactive in their coding as opposed to finding out they were hacked and immediately becoming reactive.

In this section, we'll review common security practices in the industry you can use to protect yourself so that you know what your system is doing and are not exposing too much to the world. We'll learn about the different types of logs, how to update libraries and frameworks, and how to remove header information. We'll finish this chapter by learning how to encrypt Entity Framework Core database columns.

Logging

Once you've created your website, some extra features are required before you can roll out the red carpet for everyone to enjoy it.

How do you know what's going on with your website? How will you know when someone deletes a post? How about a transaction? How long does it take for your Web API to make a full trip to present data? These questions should be answered by creating audit trails and enabling general logging for your application.

Audit trails are a type of logging where you keep track of every action a user has executed in your system. Microsoft Identity should already be in place with logging code to sprinkle throughout the application.

IIS Logs are a type of audit trail. Every user accessing your system, including anonymous users, is logged through IIS. A simple log entry is shown here:

```
192.168.15.11, -, 01/01/22, 7:55:20, W3SVC2, -, 182.15.22.90, 4502,
163, 3223, 200, 0, GET, /Index, -,
```

Standard data used in an audit trail would contain the following:

- Date/time
- IP address/port
- URL
- Action taken

- The user who executed the action

- An entity state before and after the action was executed (*optional*)

General logging is carried out more at an application level as opposed to a system level. Most general logging includes data such as this:

- Date/time

- URL

- Log type (informational, warning, or error)

- A comment about the action

- Method/action/section name performing the action

- The duration of the process (*optional*)

These types of logs are essential in the API world. These logs are created by the developer and stored on a disk or in a database. Once you create a Web API, there will be moments when you'll wonder what it's doing and why it's taking so long to complete a request. Logs are windows to the system. What exactly is happening there?

When it comes to security, your logs are gold. If someone impersonates another user, you can immediately examine the logs, identify the user and IP, and take the necessary actions to prevent it from happening again. This could be done by resetting a password, disconnecting or disabling a user from logging in, or even removing the user from the system overall.

Without logging, you'll be unaware of events occurring in your system.

Keep your Framework and Libraries Current

Every developer has their favorite libraries and frameworks. With .NET, there are times when the framework requires an update to prevent possible security threats.

Once you are aware of these security updates, it's your responsibility to update the framework and/or libraries or notify someone who *can* perform the update (in case developers are not allowed to update servers) to protect against any type of threat based on the update's vulnerabilities.

Twice in my career, a .NET version had a security issue and a security update was released to be applied to the framework. The patch wasn't applied immediately. Two weeks later, there was a breach and it was concluded the breach could've been prevented if the patch was applied two weeks earlier. It was a bad day for the company.

To see whether there is a security patch for .NET, refer to the Microsoft Update Catalog at `https://www.catalog.update.microsoft.com/home.aspx`.

Always Force SSL

If a visitor arrives through an HTTP URL and not HTTPS, it's best to redirect them over to the secure portion of your site.

HTTP Strict Transport Security Protocol (HSTS) is a security enhancement specified by the web application through a response header. When the browser receives an HSTS header, it prevents the user from using untrusted or invalid certificates.

However, there are limitations to using this:

- Modern clients must support HSTS
- HSTS must establish one HTTPS connection to establish an HSTS policy
- The web application must examine every HTTP request and redirect or reject the HTTP request

To implement this in your code, you must revisit the middleware and add the HSTS extension to a production environment. If you've just created a new web app, this is automatically added by default. Here is an example:

```
var builder = WebApplication.CreateBuilder(args);

builder.Services.AddRazorPages();

var app = builder.Build();

if (!app.Environment.IsDevelopment())
{
    app.UseExceptionHandler("/Error");
    app.UseHsts();
}

app.UseHttpsRedirection();
app.UseStaticFiles();

app.UseRouting();

app.UseAuthorization();

app.MapRazorPages();

app.Run();
```

The app.UseHttpsRedirection() method must appear after the app.UseHsts() extension method for the redirect to occur. This ensures your users will be visiting an SSL-enabled website.

Never Trust the Client

I've always likened this approach with the old saying, "Wearing suspenders with a belt." At least you wouldn't be caught with your pants down (as I use this as a security metaphor).

As mentioned near the beginning of this chapter, the intent here is to validate and sanitize data that's been submitted by the client as best you can with JavaScript and HTML and then follow up with additional validation using C# when a form is submitted.

For example, HTML 5 is now available in almost every browser, with the ability to apply a certain type to a text input, such as `type="number"` or `type="date"`. A welcome addition to this collection of input types is the ability to add a regex pattern to make validation even easier on the client side:

```
<input type="text"
       placeholder="Enter a Columbus Phone Number"
       title="Enter either a 740 or 614 area code using this format:
(740) 999-9999"
       pattern="^\(?(740|614)\)?(\s+)?[0-9]{3}-?[0-9]{4}$"
       required />
```

This pattern allows for either 740 or 614 area codes to be in a phone number. If the pattern doesn't match, you will receive a tooltip message stating why it's not valid:

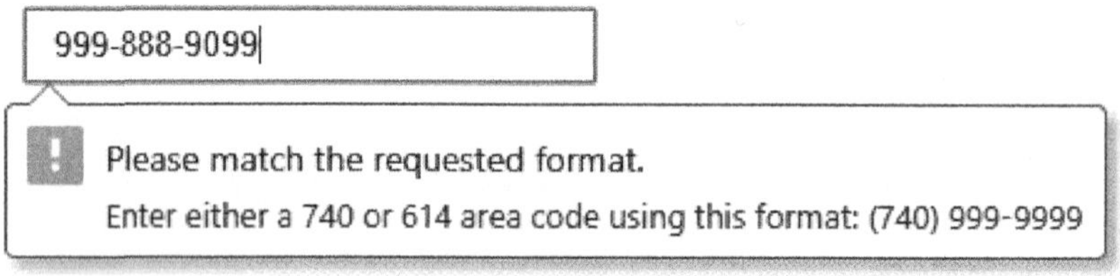

999-888-9099|

❗ Please match the requested format.
Enter either a 740 or 614 area code using this format: (740) 999-9999

Figure 4.1 – The effect of a failed validation on an input

However, this does not justify neglecting validation on the server. For every field where a user inputs data, this same effort regarding validation should be applied when the server receives the data.

Always Encode User Input

One of the easiest methods of sanitizing user input on the server is **encoding**.

If a user enters data and the data will be displayed on a page at any time, it's best to encode the data to prevent XSS. The easiest way to encode user input is to dependency inject `HtmlEncoder` into a method to perform the encoding, as shown in the following code snippet:

```
public async Task<IActionResult> OnGet(
    [FromServices] HtmlEncoder htmlEncoder,
    string q = "")
```

[handwritten margin note: Injection in the method]

```
    {
            PageResults = await PerformTheSearch(htmlEncoder.Encode(q));

            return Page();
    }
```

.NET has various injectable services already defined. `HtmlEncoder` is one such service and is injected automatically by adding a `[FromServices]` attribute. Once we have our encoder, we can encode the string that's been passed in and safely perform the action that's been requested.

In this section, you learned how to encode user input from the client, making your site safe from malicious data.

In the next section, you'll learn how to hide what your servers are telling the world and how to make a reusable middleware component.

Securing Your Headers

By default, several headers are added to HTTP requests to identify a server, the version used, what technology stack you're using, and what powers your website. While these default headers are helpful, some of them aren't required, while others can make your site more secure.

In this section, we'll focus on securing the recommended header changes through ASP.NET's Middleware.

Removing Server Headers

It's generally not a good idea to announce to the world what server you're running and its version to an anonymous user. This exposes the type of web server you're running and allows attackers to find IIS-specific techniques to gain access to your web server.

In ASP.NET, you can disable the server header for Kestrel (which is the open source server used in ASP.NET) in `Program.cs`:

```
var builder = WebApplication.CreateBuilder(args);
builder.WebHost.UseKestrel(options => options.AddServerHeader =
false);
```

When we set `AddServerHeader` to `false`, the header doesn't display the type and version of the server.

In addition to the server header, we also need to remove the `X-Powered-By` header to avoid exposing too much information. This can be achieved through middleware, as shown here:

```
app.Use(async (context, next) =>
{
    context.Response.Headers.Remove("Server");
```

```
      context.Response.Headers.Remove("X-Powered-By");
      await next();
});
```

However, you'll also have to add it to web.config, which should exist in the root of your project. Here are the only reasons web.config should exist in your project:

- Compression configuration
- Removing specific IIS headers
- Custom MIME mappings

If it doesn't exist, add it to your project and add the following path to remove the X-Powered-By header:

```xml
<?xml version="1.0" encoding="UTF-8"?>
<configuration>
  <system.webServer>
    <httpProtocol>
      <customHeaders>
        <remove name="X-Powered-By" />
```

Other header values to remove include X-Aspnet-Version and X-AspnetMvc-Version. The reason you should remove these headers is that they provide detailed information about what technology you're running on your server. If there is a security flaw specifically for ASP.NET or ASP. NET Core MVC, these headers would make your site easier for attackers to narrow down their attacks and cause an inevitable security event.

To remove these two headers, add the following two lines to the middleware in your Program.cs file:

```
context.Response.Headers.Remove("X-Aspnet-version");
context.Response.Headers.Remove("X-AspnetMvc-version");
```

No Sniffing Allowed

When you include X-Content-Type-Options in a header, this tells the browser to adhere to the MIME types registered in the Content-Type headers. These shouldn't be changed or followed:

```
context.Response.Headers.Add("X-Content-Type-Options", new
    StringValues("nosniff"));
```

This marker tells the browser that these MIME types were intentionally configured to avoid MIME-type sniffing. This helps prevent attacks based on MIME-type confusion, where non-MIME types could be considered valid MIME types.

No Framing Either

When the browser sees an X-Frame-Options header response, it indicates whether or not the browser should render the web page in <frame>, <iframe>, <embed>, or <object>:

```
context.Response.Headers.Add("X-Frame-Options", new
    StringValues("DENY"));
```

The X-Frame-Options header prevents clickjacking attacks, where someone could embed your content into other sites using frames, embeds, or objects. Setting this to DENY protects you from such attacks.

Creating a security middleware component

To finalize this section, we'll create a simple middleware component we can reuse in our .NET Core web applications.

Since we created our middleware skeleton in *Chapter 3*, we can reuse the code for our RemoveInsecureHeadersMiddleware component, as shown here:

```
public class RemoveInsecureHeadersMiddleware
{
    private readonly RequestDelegate _next;

    public RemoveInsecureHeadersMiddleware(RequestDelegate next)
    {
        _next = next;
    }

    public async Task Invoke(HttpContext httpContext)
    {
        httpContext.Response.OnStarting((state) =>
        {
            httpContext.Response.Headers.Remove("Server");
            httpContext.Response.Headers.Remove("X-Powered-By");
            httpContext.Response.Headers.Remove("X-Aspnet-version");
            httpContext.Response.Headers.Remove("X-AspnetMvc-
                version");

            httpContext.Response.Headers.Add("X-Content-Type-Options",
                new StringValues("nosniff"));

            httpContext.Response.Headers.Add("X-Frame-Options",
                new StringValues("DENY"));
```

```
            return Task.CompletedTask;
        }, null!);

        await _next(httpContext);
    }
}
```

Don't forget our extension method:

```
public static class RemoveInsecureHeadersMiddlewareExtensions
{
    public static IApplicationBuilder RemoveInsecureHeaders(
        this IApplicationBuilder builder)
    {
        return builder.
UseMiddleware<RemoveInsecureHeadersMiddleware>();
    }
}
```

We can use newly created security extension in our `Program.cs` file:

```
app.RemoveInsecureHeaders();
```

While we've added the most obvious headers, the good news is that you can update this component by adding additional headers to increase the security of your site even further.

In this section, you learned how to secure your headers and create a reusable middleware component for all of your web applications. In the next section, you'll learn how to secure Entity Framework by encrypting your data, using stored procedures, and using parameterized queries.

Securing Entity Framework Core

Entity Framework Core is one of those technologies that continues to amaze me. Every version of Entity Framework Core that's released provides some new performance enhancement, a better approach to a technique, or some other method to make our lives a little bit easier.

In this section, we'll learn about how we can encrypt our data at the database level.

Encrypting Your Data

One of the most valuable things to a company is data. To prevent an attack, one of the security measures you can take is to encrypt the data in the table.

At the beginning of this chapter, we explained the types of data that require special attention, such as phone numbers, email addresses, and credit card data.

The best approach is to apply security at the database level by using the database's encryption technology, whether it's SQL Server or a similar database.

SQL Server encrypts specific columns by using the **Encrypt Columns…** option in **SQL Server Management Studio** (**SSMS**), as shown in *Figure 4.2*:

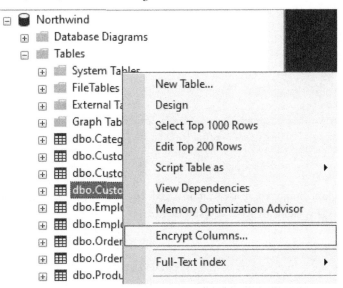

Figure 4.2 – The Encrypt Columns… option in SQL Server Management Studio

If you are using Entity Framework, generating a DbContext will take the secure columns into account. Again, when creating encryption at the database level, it would be another roadblock to dissuade attackers from accessing sensitive data.

In this section, we examined the best approach to protecting your data – that is, by encrypting your data using SQL Server's **Encrypt Columns…** feature. In the next section, we'll look at how to protect your pages from a **cross-site request forgery** (**XSRF**) attack.

Use Microsoft Entra for Securing Applications

As mentioned previously, when logging into a website, it's best to protect the database from intruders by encrypting the database. This means using existing methods as opposed to writing custom encryption algorithms. Creating a custom encryption algorithm should be avoided since most algorithms are easily broken through hacker tools. It's best to use an existing framework like Microsoft Identity (now called Entra).

With Blazor and SPAs (Single-Page Applications) all the rage, it can be hard to secure an application using APIs. Previously, using Microsoft Identity through an API required a lot of effort making it harder to implement secure applications.

With the latest .NET 8, Microsoft Entra introduces API-based calls for every aspect of security for web applications for **Single-Page Applications (SPAs)**. When creating a new application, the following code adds an Entra-enabled REST-based API to an application:

```
var builder = WebApplication.CreateBuilder(args);

// Add services to the container.
builder.Services
    .AddAuthentication(JwtBearerDefaults.AuthenticationScheme)
    .AddMicrosoftIdentityWebApi(builder.Configuration.
GetSection("AzureAd"));
builder.Services.AddAuthorization();
```

The preceding code creates our web application and defines a JwtBearerDefault authentication scheme and adds a Web API specifically for Microsoft Identity.

If JWT Tokens are not an option, .NET 8 also introduces Bearer Tokens as shown here:

```
var builder = WebApplication.CreateBuilder(args);

// Add services to the container.
builder.Services
    .AddAuthentication()
    .AddBearerToken();
builder.Services.AddAuthorization();
```

The ability to write fast APIs along with simple authentication and authorization gives web developers more options when writing web applications using Blazor and SPAs. We'll cover Microsoft Entra more in *Chapter 9* when looking at creating better web APIs.

Protecting Your Pages with Anti-Forgery

Cross-site request forgery, or XSRF, is where an attack occurs, tricking a user to execute unwanted actions in a web application in which they're currently authenticated. For example, a user could be tricked into using their credit card on a different site without them even knowing it.

To prevent an XSRF attack through your web forms, the recommended approach is to use anti-forgery tokens.

To add some to our Middleware, we will add them to our pipeline, as shown in the following code snippet:

```
services.AddAntiforgery();
```

When an HTML form is created, anti-forgery tokens are automatically generated when a `<form>` tag contains `method="post"` and one of the following conditions is true:

- The action attribute is empty (`action=""`)
- The action attribute isn't supplied (`<form method="post">`)

If you have other attributes attached to the form tag, you can explicitly add an `HtmlHelper` called `AntiForgeryToken()` inside the form tag:

```
@Html.AntiForgeryToken();
```

This will generate a hidden input with an arbitrary value. If the value that comes back from the client is not the same as when the server originally sent it, the request will be denied.

In this section, you learned about audit trails and general logging, how to keep your frameworks and libraries current, how to always force SSL to make your connections secure, and to never trust the client's input. You also learned that every user input should be encoded when received by the server, how to secure your headers, how to secure your database by using Entity Framework Core, and, finally, how to protect your forms from cross-site request forgery attacks by using the `.AddAntiForgery()` Middleware service.

In the next section, we'll look at some real-world issues and how to solve the top three threats according to OWASP.

Safeguarding Against the Top 3 Security Threats

The Open Worldwide Application Security Project, or OWASP, is a non-profit foundation dedicated to improving the security of software. Since new threats are emerging all the time, they keep a list called the OWASP Top 10, which is meant to keep software developers up to date regarding the latest security threats and how to prevent them. The Top 10 list includes the following security threats:

1. Broken Access Control
2. Cryptographic Failures
3. Injection
4. Insecure Design
5. Security Misconfiguration
6. Vulnerable and Outdated Components
7. Identification and Authentication Failures

8. Software and Data Integrity Failures

9. Security Logging and Monitoring Failures

10. **Server-Side Request Forgery (SSRF)**

In this section, we'll cover the top three threats and how to safeguard your ASP.NET Core application from these threats – that is, Broken Access Control, Cryptographic Failures, and Injection.

Broken Access Control

Broken access control is when a user can perform a particular act in the system outside of their intended permissions. Permission checks could be missing in the software, or the correct permissions might not have been checked in the software.

The key word to focus on here is **authorization**. Authorizing users into your system is a big responsibility.

Let's look at how to get better at access control.

Denying Access by Default

When someone visits a site, consider them anonymous and restricted from the administrative area. When an administrator adds someone to the system, they are now authenticated and should be able to log in to the system.

Your authorization system should be thoroughly tested. Even though a user is allowed to log in, they shouldn't be able to do anything unless an administrator authorizes them.

"Deny by default" means that when a user uses the system, they should be denied access until permissions are granted.

For Razor Pages, you can use the `.AddRazorPages()` Middleware component configuration to authorize certain pages and folders, as shown in the following code snippet:

```
services.AddRazorPages(options =>
{
    options.Conventions.AuthorizeAreaFolder("Admin", "/Areas/Admin");
    options.Conventions.AllowAnonymousToFolder("/");
});
```

In the `AddRazorPages` method, we are only allowing authenticated users into the `Admin` area; anonymous users can only go to the root of the website.

For controller-based pages such as ASP.NET MVC, you can use the `[Authorize]` attribute to allow authenticated users to view the page, as shown here:

```
[Authorize]
public class MySecretController : Controller
```

```
{
    public ActionResult Index()
    {
    }
}
```

In the preceding code, the Index page isn't available to the authenticated user because the [Authorize] attribute is on MySecretController.

If you only want the Index page to be available to authenticated users, put the [Authorize] attribute on the Index() method, as shown here:

```
[Authorize]
public ActionResult Index()
{
}
```

These techniques deny anonymous users by default, which should be the proper approach.

Avoid Exposing Keys

 NO Int IDS AS QS

When you're building a blog, it's best to have a URL without a post ID as an integer. When I've written blog posts, I've seen hits on my page before the page was public. It was great to see people were interested in looking at my latest post, but how were they getting to it? They would go to my blog, pull up the latest post, and add 1 to the post ID. There it was – an unfinished post in all its unfinished glory.

Imagine this type of scenario on a bank website. A user logs in to their account and they see the following URL: https://www.bobsbank.com/view/accountid=511324.

A curious user could add 1 to the account ID and view another person's account.

Avoid exposing accounts or primary keys to users and, if a user does guess an account number, confirm the authenticated user is the owner of their account before viewing it.

Final Notes on Broken Access Controls

Here are some other things you should consider:

- Audit trails and logs are gold. They will help you identify risks and patterns with users.
- Confirm your authorization system works by running unit tests and integration tests. We'll cover unit and integration tests in a later chapter.

In this section, we learned how to protect ourselves from broken access controls by denying users by default, hiding primary keys, and protecting certain pages by confirming users are allowed to view that page, as well as how to implement audit trails and logs and battle-test our authorization system.

In this next section, we'll look at how to protect against cryptographic failures.

Cryptographic Failures

OWASP considers cryptographic failures as sensitive data that is unencrypted, failed security measures that use invalid access control, and even stale server environments, such as servers that don't contain the latest security patches. This includes using industry-proven encryption algorithms which are already included in Microsoft Entra.

The following sections detail more common incidents in the industry.

Transmitting Clear Text

If you are transmitting sensitive data across the wire, it should be encrypted by using an SSL connection.

 A general rule of thumb is that the client should be the one sending sensitive data to the server, not the other way around.

If you need to send sensitive data back to the client for approval, it's best to mask the data somehow for display purposes (for example, using XXXX-XXXX-XXXX-9999 for credit cards) and, when updated, confirm this by having the authenticated user re-enter their password or providing some way to authenticate them again.

Invalid/Expired SSL Certificates

Once your code gets to a server, its primary job is to deliver the data as fast and as securely as possible.

Certificates are required for SSL to create secure connections that have an expiration date. There should be some reminder or notification letting administrators know when a certificate expires. It's not recommended to continue using an expired certificate on your site.

Unencrypted Database

Again, if your database contains sensitive information, it's best to be proactive and encrypt the database using the database's recommended encryption method.

Final Notes on Cryptographic Failures

Let's look at some final notes:

- Avoid weak algorithms such as MD5, SHA1, or PKCS number 1 v1.5, which are easy algorithms to break.
- Avoid sending sensitive data to the client. If this is necessary, mask the data.
- Use proper access key management, storing keys in safe locations such as Microsoft's Key Vault, Google's Cloud Key Management, or Amazon's Key Management Service.

In this section, we learned how to avoid cryptographic failures by avoiding sending clear text, updating stale or invalid SSL certificates, and always encrypting the database if it contains sensitive data.

In the final section, we'll look at how injection can impact your application.

Injection

In 2017, OWASP reported SQL injection was the top threat when writing code for the web. Now, their Top 10 includes simply "injection," which is an umbrella term covering SQL injection and XSS as well.

SQL Injection

We already mentioned that you should never trust the client and always sanitize and encode user input, but it bears repeating since it is still considered a threat, even if it did move down two spots to number three.

The great news is that Entity Framework Core supports parameterized queries to help you avoid SQL injection. However, this feature doesn't mean you don't have to sanitize input from users.

Script Injection

Script injection is when someone enters a script tag in a text box and the value is accepted and saved in the database. When the data is displayed on the page, the script is triggered and performs a particular action.

Here is a simple extension method that searches for and destroys malicious tags from HTML using regex:

```
public static class StringExtensions
{
    public static string Sanitize(this string content)
    {
        // Replace the malicious tags with nothing.
        var maliciousTagsPattern =
            @"<(applet|embed|frameset|head|noframes|noscript|object|
            form|select|option|script|style|title)(.*?)>"+
            "((.|\n)*?)"+
            "</(applet|embed|frameset|head|noframes|noscript|object|
            select|form|option|script|style|title)>";
        var options = RegexOptions.IgnoreCase | RegexOptions.
            Multiline;
        var regex = new Regex(maliciousTagsPattern, options);
        content = regex.Replace(content, @"");

        // Remove the Javascript function on the tags (i.e.
            OnChange="Javascript:<blah blah blah>")
        var inlinePattern = @"<[^>]*=""javascript:[^""]*""[^>]*>";
```

```
        options = RegexOptions.IgnoreCase;
        var regex2 = new Regex(inlinePattern, options);

        return regex2.Replace(content, @"");
    }
}
```

While this .Sanitize() extension method removes any malicious tags from a string, if you are passing in HTML-formatted text, it also removes any tag using any JavaScript events on tags (such as onclick='alert("gotcha");'). It then returns the sanitized string for use.

Use this extension method like any other extension method with a string:

```
var sanitizedString = inputFromUser.Sanitize();
```

You could even extend the method further so that it includes other safeguards, such as encoding the string before returning it.

Always validate, filter, and sanitize input from the user. No matter what.

Final Notes on Injection

Here are some final things you should consider:

- The further you can keep users (and users with malicious intent) away from the database, the better

- Confirm you have a maxlength attribute on single-line inputs to minimize how many characters are acceptable and limit the ability to allow scripts in HTML input fields

Injection continues to be a credible threat and has always been listed on OWASP's Top 10 list.

Summary

In this chapter, we learned how to safeguard our code by understanding what sensitive data is and how to secure it using authentication, authorization, and SSL-enabled connections.

In the second part of this chapter, we reviewed some common standards in the industry, such as logging, keeping our frameworks and libraries up-to-date, and always redirecting to SSL-enabled sites. After that, we learned to never trust client data and that we should validate, filter, and sanitize it and always encode it, and not announce to the world what server and version we're running by adding or removing security headers. We even created a reusable security middleware component.

We also touched on encrypting database columns with SQL Server and how it's important to protect fields by being proactive, and why creating a custom encryption algorithm should be avoided.. We also learned how to avoid cross-site request forgery by using anti-forgery tokens.

Finally, we examined the top three threats as determined by the OWASP Foundation and how to properly protect ourselves from Broken Access Control, Cryptographic Failures, and Injection of all types.

In the next chapter, we'll pick up the discussion of Entity Framework Core once more and learn how to optimize data access using Entity Framework Core by using some intuitive techniques.

5

Optimizing Data Access with Entity Framework Core

Before Entity Framework was introduced in 2008, developers used **ActiveX Data Objects (ADOs)** and **Object Linking and Embedding Database (OLE DB)** to access their data for applications. Since its introduction, Entity Framework has evolved over the years into a high-performance bridge between **object-oriented (OO)** systems and relational databases. It enables developers to use **Language Integrated Query (LINQ)** syntax to perform complex queries using C#. However, some LINQ statements can be overwhelming for new developers. Since this is one of the most discussed topics when it comes to data access, we'll cover various standards and implementations when using Entity Framework Core.

This chapter will be similar to *Chapter 2, CI/CD – Building Quality Software with Software*, where we will review patterns for implementing Entity Framework Core to access data but also look at some common uses of Entity Framework Core in the industry.

In this chapter, we'll cover the following main topics:

- Entity Framework Core Implementations
- Common Entity Framework Core Practices
- Implementing the Theme Park Example

When you've finished reading this chapter, you'll have a better understanding of the various design patterns and approaches you can use with Entity Framework Core and the various standards involved; we will end the chapter by applying these standards to a theme park example.

Let's get started by examining the various Entity Framework Core common implementations used by many developers.

Technical requirements

I recommend using your favorite editor to view the GitHub repository. Our recommendations include the following:

- Visual Studio (preferably 2022 or newer)
- Visual Studio Code
- JetBrains Rider

The editor we'll be using is Visual Studio Enterprise 2022, but any version (Community or Professional) will work with the code.

We will also be using **SQL Server Management Studio** (**SSMS**) for our example at the end of the chapter. However, if you feel you don't need to download another tool, you can view SQL Server data through Visual Studio 2022 as well without installing SSMS.

> **Downloading SQL Server Developer Edition**
>
> To run a local copy of SQL Server, download the Developer edition of SQL Server from `https://www.microsoft.com/en-us/sql-server/sql-server-downloads`.

The code for this chapter is located in Packt Publishing's GitHub repository, which you can navigate to here: `https://github.com/PacktPublishing/ASP.NET-Core-8-Best-Practices`.

Entity Framework Core Implementations

Over the years, developers have used Entity Framework Core in various ways. Some were exceptionally **creative**.

In this section, we'll discuss the following architectural approaches:

- Repository/Unit of Work
- Specification
- Extension Methods

While these implementations are based on real-world experiences, they are merely observations, and, as mentioned in *Chapter 1*, the decision will fall on teams and/or community members as to the right approach for the application and trade-offs incurred.

Repository/Unit of Work

While this implementation has already caused some friction among developers, it's a common pattern seen with early adopters of ASP.NET Entity Framework applications (including me). However, it's been said by community members it's not an efficient way to use Entity Framework architecturally because of the duplication of repositories.

Implementation

Out of the box, the DbContext follows a **repository** and **unit of work** design pattern.

The repository design pattern is a class that manages objects between the business domain and the mapping of properties from the database using lists and single domain objects.

Repositories are self-contained in the DbContext, which is considered a Unit of Work design pattern. A unit of work pattern manages a list of objects (as repositories do) using a ChangeTracker to track changes in a transaction-like state and organizes how each change should be saved and how to resolve concurrency problems.

In Entity Framework, repositories are represented as DbSet instances in the DbContext where the DbContext is the unit of work itself.

Let's look at an example. We have a database called ThemePark and it contains two tables: attractions and locations. We've also created a ThemeParkDbContext class to manage our entities. If you've worked with Entity Framework at any time, you've likely encountered the repository design pattern implemented in a similar fashion:

```csharp
public class AttractionRepository
{
    private readonly ThemeParkDbContext _context;

    public AttractionRepository(ThemeParkDbContext context)
    {
        _context = context;
    }

    public List<Attraction> GetAttractions()
    {
        return _context.Attractions.ToList();
    }

    public Attraction GetAttraction(int id)
    {
        return _context.Attractions.FirstOrDefault(e => e.Id == id,
            null);
    }
}
```

What is wrong with this implementation? While this does separate the business rules from the data access, it's an unnecessary layer for applications when a repository layer already exists in the DbContext.

One of the jokes I love from the developer community is, *"What are the two hardest problems in computer science? Cache invalidation, naming things, and off-by-one errors."*

Consider this a case of naming things wrong. What if we changed the name to Service, like so?

```
public class AttractionService
{
    private readonly ThemeParkDbContext _context;

    public AttractionService(ThemeParkDbContext context)
    {
        _context = context;
    }
}
```

Why Service? The repository pattern is already contained in the DbContext as a DbSet<Attraction>. The service uses the repository pattern to retrieve the data and perform additional updates before returning the data. Changing the class name from Repository to Service signifies we don't need a repository pattern on top of an already existing repository. When creating a service for individual repositories (DbSet instances), this provides multiple benefits, as follows:

1. **Logically partitioning data access**—While we're isolating a repository to one service, that doesn't mean we won't need related entities from the DbContext. Add .Include() on the DbContext to retrieve related entities.

2. **Flexibility**—The service dependency injects a DbContext instance through the constructor, allowing for multiple approaches to accessing data including LINQ statements, stored procedures, or even call raw SQL.

3. **Additional processing**—When calling a data access service, there are times when the data requires more massaging before returning the results. While this is temporarily acceptable in this service, it may require refactoring to the appropriate business entity or processing through another class.

The benefits seen through this approach could easily pivot the already existing repository naming convention to a service moniker.

The Specification Pattern

Developers are always looking to reuse existing code and make it as flexible as possible for maintenance purposes; update a line of code and it could change the retrieval of data required.

The specification pattern is solving the problem of attaching requirements to an object with the rise of **Test-Driven Development** (**TDD**) making it easier to understand the results retrieved through a query. It uses a base class to retrieve data as either a list or a single entity while writing the least amount of code.

Implementation

When creating a specification class, you need two classes: one for processing the request and the specification for what you need. The specification class is built exactly as the class implies: it defines the filter for a single entity or list of entities, sorting and grouping, and inclusion of various related entities. Everything you can do with a LINQ query can be defined in the specification class.

A sample specification's contract (interface) could have the following structure:

```
public interface ISpecification<T>
{
    Expression<Func<T, bool>> Filter { get; }

    Expression<Func<T, object>> OrderBy { get; }

    Expression<Func<T, object>> OrderByDescending { get; }

    List<Expression<Func<T, object>>> Includes { get; }

    Expression<Func<T, object>> GroupBy { get; }
}
```

The implementation of a `Specification` class would look like this:

```
public class Specification<TEntity>: ISpecification<TEntity> where
TEntity: class
{
    public Expression<Func<TEntity, bool>> Filter { get; }
    public Expression<Func<TEntity, object>> OrderBy { get; set; } =
        null!;
    public Expression<Func<TEntity, object>> OrderByDescending { get;
        set; } = null!;
    public Expression<Func<TEntity, object>> GroupBy { get; set; } =
        null!;
    public List<Expression<Func<TEntity, object>>> Includes { get; } =
        null!;

    public Specification(Expression<Func<TEntity, bool>> filter)
    {
        Filter = filter;
    }
}
```

As mentioned at the start of this section, the properties in the class represent all of the different aspects of retrieving data: filtering, including, sorting, and grouping.

Once you have the specification defined, we need a way to build our query based on a specification. In this case, we'll create a `SpecificationBuilder<T>` class:

```
public static class SpecificationBuilder<TEntity> where TEntity: class
{
    public static IQueryable<TEntity> GetQuery(IQueryable<TEntity>
inputQuery,
        ISpecification<TEntity> specification)
    {
        var query = inputQuery;

        if (specification == null)
        {
            return query;
        }

        if (specification.Filter != null)
        {
            query = query.Where(specification.Filter);
        }

        if (specification.Includes != null
            && specification.Includes.Any())
        {
            foreach (var include in specification.Includes)
            {
                query = query.Include(include);
            }
        }

        if (specification.OrderBy != null)
        {
            query = query
                .OrderBy(specification.OrderBy);
        }
        else if (specification.OrderByDescending != null)
        {
            query = query
                .OrderByDescending(specification.OrderByDescending);
        }
```

```
        if (specification.GroupBy != null)
        {
            query = query
                .GroupBy(specification.GroupBy)
                .SelectMany(x => x);
        }


        return query;
    }
}
```

In the preceding code snippet, our `SpecificationBuilder` class creates a LINQ query to retrieve the data. Since everything is self-contained and completely independent of itself, the class was marked as static.

With every specification class, we need a way to retrieve the data. We'll make the class abstract and call it `BaseSpecificationService<TEntity>`:

```
public abstract class BaseSpecificationService<TEntity> where TEntity
: class
{
    private readonly ThemeParkDbContext _context;

    protected BaseSpecificationService(ThemeParkDbContext context)
    {
        _context = context;
    }

    protected ISpecification<TEntity> Specification { get; set; } =
        null!;

    protected IQueryable<TEntity> GetQuery()
    {
        return SpecificationBuilder<TEntity>
            .GetQuery(_context.Set<TEntity>().AsQueryable(),
                Specification);
    }
}
```

In the preceding code, `BaseSpecificationService` is what we'll use to create our specific data needs. We require a specification property and a way to retrieve the query based on that specification.

With the specification pattern, the names of your classes are the specifications of the data required.

Let's look at another example with a simple `Product` class:

```
public class Product
{
    public string Name { get; private set; }
    public int Price { get; private set; }
}
```

If you need a list of all products below $5.00, a specification class would look like the following:

```
public class GetProductsLessThanFiveDollars :
BaseSpecificationService<Product>
{
    public GetProductsLessThanFiveDollars(InventoryDbContext context)
: base(context)
    {
        Specification = new Specification<Product>(product => product.
Price <= 5);
    }
}
```

This code creates the specification and uses it to retrieve the results:

```
var productsBelowFiveDollarsSpecification = new
GetProductsLessThanFiveDollars(_context);
var results = productsBelowFiveDollarsSpecification.GetQuery().
ToList();
```

The preceding code would generate a list of products of less than 5 dollars.

While this is a simple example, there are more extensive libraries dedicated to this type of Entity Framework design pattern, such as Steve Smith's specification library located at `https://specification.ardalis.com`.

Extension Methods

If we revisit the repository/unit of work method, the association between specific business logic and the data should be relatively close to `DbContext`. Instead of creating service classes while passing `DbContext` in, why not just attach your data access to the actual `DbSet` instance itself as an `IQueryable` extension method?

The ability to add specific calls to a `DbContext` or `DbSet` instance is extremely attractive because they can be placed anywhere in your project.

The extension method approach does require a bit of discipline where specific entities are concerned. For example, if you created a product entity, your `IQueryable` extension methods should return only products and not order entities. Mixing order extension methods with product extension methods is usually frowned upon.

Implementation

Extension methods allow your code to be more direct when accessing data.

Since we can attach extension methods to interfaces, let's define a simple interface for our ThemeParkDbContext class, as follows:

```
public interface IThemeParkDbContext
{
    DbSet<Attraction> Attractions { get; set; }
    DbSet<Location> Locations { get; set; }
    DbSet<TEntity> Set<TEntity>() where TEntity : class;
    DatabaseFacade Database { get; }
}
```

With our theme park idea, we built AttractionExtensions and LocationExtensions files for data access, like so:

```
public static class AttractionExtensions
{
    public static List<Attraction> GetAttractions(this
IThemeParkDbContext context)
    {
        return context.Attractions.ToList();
    }


    public static Attraction GetAttraction(this IThemeParkDbContext
context, int id)
    {
        return context.Attractions
            .Include(t => t.Location)
            .FirstOrDefault(e => e!.Id == id, null)!;
    }
}
```

Our AttractionExtensions file has only two methods, GetAttractions() and GetAttraction(), which we attach to the ThemeParkDbContext class.

Our LocationExtensions file is small and compact as well, as we can see here:

```
public static class LocationExtensions
{
    public static List<Location> GetLocations(this IThemeParkDbContext
context)
    {
        return context.Locations.ToList();
```

```
    }

    public static Location GetLocation(this IThemeParkDbContext
context, int id)
    {
        return context.Locations.FirstOrDefault(e => e!.Id == id,
null)!;
    }
}
```

In this section, we reviewed some of the more common Entity Framework Core design patterns used in real-world applications such as the repository and unit of work patterns, the specification pattern, and the extension methods approach to accessing data.

While these are common in the .NET community, there are other patterns available for Entity Framework Core allowing even easier access to your data, but they do have drawbacks. Let's look at these more closely:

- **Partitioned DbContext instances**—One DbContext instance would exist for each partitioned feature in the application; for example, one DbContext instance for the Books and BookAuthors tables and another DbContext instance for the Orders and Books tables. One drawback is possible state conflicts across multiple DbContext instances (*NOT* recommended).

- **Stored procedures**—Using a DbContext instance as a conduit while making direct calls to stored procedures without using LINQ. One drawback occurs when changes are made to a stored procedure and the mapping code doesn't reflect the results returned, causing an error.

In the next section, we'll be covering some common practices when using Entity Framework Core in real-world applications.

Common Entity Framework Core Practices

Even though Entity Framework patterns provide additional structure to your code, there are also common practices to keep in mind when building applications with Entity Framework.

In this section, we'll review some of the more common uses of Entity Framework and their benefits: how async/await can make your application more scalable, logging your queries to optimize SQL output, creating resource files to hold seed data for tables, learning about deferred execution, speeding up access with a read-only method called .AsNoTracking(), leveraging the database where it makes sense, and using AutoMapper to map source objects to destination objects.

Confirming Your Model

If you're using the database-first approach (where you have an existing database to work with) to generate your models, confirm that all of your indexes, relationships, identity fields, and foreign keys represent your model accordingly before using Scaffold-DbContext. The Scaffold-Database command creates your DbContext instance based on an existing database. The command takes everything into account when creating the DbContext instance.

If your relationships aren't correct, this will cause problems with navigation properties on your model when accessing them through your DbContext instance. Essentially, your navigation properties will be empty.

Using Async/Await

For I/O-bound activities, such as database operations, it makes sense to use async/await for creating scalable applications. While it may not be apparent when running the web application on a developer machine, the true benefits of using async/await appear when you have hundreds of people hitting the website at once.

The reason to use async/await is to avoid blocking thread requests. When a request comes into a web server, the .NET Framework maintains a pool of threads to process those incoming requests. For each request, a thread is taken from the pool and used to process the request synchronously. While the thread is being used, nothing can use it until the process is completed ("blocking thread"). Once the process completes, the thread is released and returned to the thread pool for the next request.

When you use async/await, you aren't taking a thread from the thread pool. Anything in between async and await doesn't use a thread, which means you're saving memory in the long run and allowing your application to perform better.

When it comes to making Entity Framework Core calls, it's best to use async/await for performance reasons.

Logging Your Queries

Most **Database Administrators (DBA)** are averse to programmers using Entity Framework mainly because it allows ad hoc queries to be passed to the database and executed immediately. The reason for this is that most feel Entity Framework is a black box and can't see what's happening behind the scenes. A method was added to the OptionsBuilder class specifically for logging to help solve this issue.

For simple logging using Entity Framework, place a .LogTo() method into your DbContext instance's onConfiguring() method, as shown in the following code snippet:

```
    protected override void OnConfiguring(DbContextOptionsBuilder
optionsBuilder)
    {
```

```
      if (!optionsBuilder.IsConfigured)
      {
          optionsBuilder.LogTo(Console.WriteLine);
      }
  }
```

The .LogTo() method takes either an action or a func on where to send the log data. In this snippet, we are simply logging to the debug window.

Simple logging to the debug window is the easiest to implement because it's a simple Console. Write() method and doesn't require any third-party packages, but there are other types of logging available that are just as easy to plug into Entity Framework Core.

Additional logging options

For additional logging methods in Entity Framework Core, navigate to the following URL: https://learn.microsoft.com/en-us/ef/core/logging-events-diagnostics/.

Using Resources for Large Seed Data

If you need initial seed data with fewer than 20 records for your tables, it's easy to just hand-code the records on the fly in your DbContext instance using .HasData().

But what if you have a table requiring hundreds of records seeded on the initial load? Hand-typing records can be painful using code.

One hidden gem in .NET is the use of resource files for storing simple strings (normally used for localization/translation), but it can also be used for populating seed data.

Let's use our Attraction/Location table example and show the steps for creating seed data in a resource file:

1. Open SQL Server Management Studio.

2. Confirm the seeded records are created the way you want them in each table (Attraction and Location).

3. Perform a SELECT operation with the JSON clause added to the end, as shown in the following SQL snippet:

```
    SELECT
          [ID]
        , [Name]
        , [LocationID]
```

```
FROM [dbo].Attraction
FOR JSON AUTO, INCLUDE_NULL_VALUES
```

4. Click on the result, and a new result pane will open with your JSON. The JSON will look like this:

```
[{
        "ID": 1,
        "Name": "Twirly Ride",
        "LocationID": 2
    }, {
        "ID": 2,
        "Name": "Mine car Coaster",
        "LocationID": 5
    }, {
        "ID": 3,
        "Name": "Haunted House",
        "LocationID": 3
    }, {
        "ID": 4,
        "Name": "Dragon Ride",
        "LocationID": 2
    }, {
        "ID": 5,
        "Name": "Gift Shop",
        "LocationID": 1
    }, {
        "ID": 6,
        "Name": "Space Ride",
        "LocationID": 4
    }, {
        "ID": 7,
        "Name": "Shootout at OK Corral\/Lazer Tag",
        "LocationID": 5
    }
]
```

5. Copy the JSON returned.

6. Open Visual Studio and add a resource file through Visual Studio. The following screenshot illustrates the process:

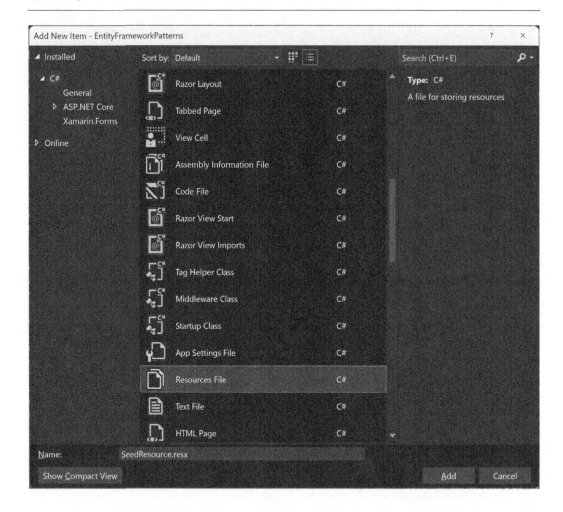

Figure 5.1 – Creating a resource file called SeedResource.resx in Visual Studio

7. Your resource file will automatically open. For our example, we'll create the resource with the following parameters:

    A. **Name**: AttractionRecords

    B. **Value**: <Paste your JSON here>

    C. **Comment**: (These are optional, but added to identify for other devs)

    D. **Access Modifier**: Change this to **Internal**

Your resource record should look like this:

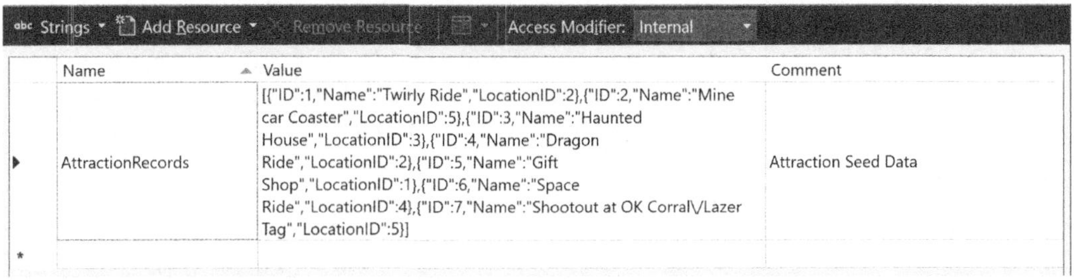

Figure 5.2 – A sample record in the Resources.resx file containing JSON for the Attraction table

8. Save your resource file.

9. Open your `AttractionConfiguration` class and locate your `.HasData()` attraction in your `DbContext` instance and replace it with the following code:

```
var records = JsonSerializer.Deserialize<Attraction[]>(
    SeedResource.AttractionRecords);
if (records != null)
{
    builder.HasData(records);
}
```

10. Save and compile your code.

If you require a large amount of seed data, it's better to create resource files with JSON data instead of hand-coding all of the records into code. Finding long pages of large JSON strings in a `DbContext` configuration may seem jarring to some developers.

Understanding Deferred Execution

Deferred execution when making Entity Framework calls means the LINQ query is delayed until the realized value is required.

Here's an example:

```
var products = this.Products.ToList().Where(r => r.CategoryId == 15);
```

While this will return the correct list of items, it's not as performant as it could be. With the `.ToList()` method added after the Products `DbSet` instance, the entire `Products` table is loaded, and *then* the `.Where()` method is executed.

A better approach to this call is shown in this code snippet:

```
var products = this.Products.Where(r => r.CategoryId == 15).ToList();
```

This will also return the correct list of products. However, the SQL query generated will contain a WHERE clause as well to filter out and return the correct list of records. The difference here is the first query will return *all* of the records from the Products table and then filter out the resulting product list using the .Where() LINQ method. Remember—LINQ can also work with arrays.

With the second query, a WHERE clause is created when the .ToList() method is encountered, and a subset of records is returned and "materialized" into entities, making this query extremely faster.

Deferred execution means you are building the query and not executing it immediately. When you are finished building your query and want the results, end your LINQ query with a .ToList() method. If you are looking for one entity, end your LINQ query with a .Single(), .SingleOrDefault(), .First(), or .FirstOrDefault() method.

Using a Read-Only State with .AsNoTracking()

When retrieving data using LINQ, the DbContext instance has something called a ChangeTracker, which is updated when an entity's state changes. This requires overhead—a small amount of overhead, but overhead, nonetheless.

If you are using DbSet in a read-only situation, use the .AsNoTracking() method at the beginning of a LINQ statement to make Entity Framework Core aware it doesn't need to track the state of models returned.

For example, the following LINQ query will retrieve an Attraction object without updating the ChangeTracker:

```
public Attraction GetAttraction(int id)
{
    return _context.Attractions
        .AsNoTracking()
        .FirstOrDefault(e => e!.Id == id, null)!;
}
```

In the previous snippet, we place the .AsNoTracking() method right after the DbSet instance, letting Entity Framework Core know not to track anything.

Leveraging the Database

While it's tempting to create everything in Entity Framework, there are times when it's better to let the database perform data-heavy operations.

With one project, I was writing large LINQ queries in code to retrieve entities into memory. Then, I continued to write code to calculate a count of items, sum up totals, and finally relate all types of child entities to the main collection of entities.

I realized I could achieve all of this using a stored procedure and bypass Entity Framework altogether. A stored procedure took care of these details, and Entity Framework Core simply retrieved the results.

Sometimes, it makes sense to let the database do the heavy lifting of calculating data and provide the results to the application since that's its job.

Avoiding the Manual Property Mapping

When sending entities to render on the client, it's best to create **Data Transfer Objects** (**DTOs**). You only want to send the minimal amount of data relevant to the currently displayed web page.

However, it gets tiring writing manual left-to-right property assignments. One recommendation is to use AutoMapper.

AutoMapper enables the automation of mapping properties from one source object to a destination object. In the following example, we are taking an `Attraction` object and copying the properties over to a new `AttractionDto` object. AutoMapper handles the heavy lifting for us by matching properties and copying the data over to the destination object:

```
var config = new MapperConfiguration(cfg =>
    cfg.CreateMap<Attraction, AttractionDto>());

IMapper mapper = new Mapper(config);
var dest = mapper.Map<Attraction, AttractionDto>(attractionObject);
```

`AutoMapper` is very flexible, fills a specific need, has been downloaded from NuGet over 400,000 times, and is used by over 100,000 developers in the industry.

AutoMapper Library

The previous functionality only scratches the surface of what AutoMapper is capable of doing for developers. To understand the full potential of AutoMapper, visit the fully documented website at the following URL: `https://docs.automapper.org/`.

In this section, we learned about the common uses of Entity Framework Core in the industry. We learned it's best to confirm your database before creating your database-first `DbContext` instance, along with leveraging the capabilities of your database instead of hand-coding everything, and about how to perform read-only queries with `.AsNoTracking()`, why it's best to use `async/await`, and why understanding deferred execution is important when writing LINQ queries. Finally, we examined how to log your queries, how to seed your tables using resource files, and avoiding manual left-to-right property mapping by using AutoMapper.

In the next section, we'll take a simple Entity Framework application and apply all of our standards, and even learn some new techniques as well.

Implementing the Theme Park Example

There is so much to digest when it comes to Entity Framework Core and all of its features. There are entire books on Entity Framework Core; this chapter will only scratch the surface.

> **Entity Framework Core Recommendation**
>
> For a deeper dive into Entity Framework Core, I would recommend Mastering Entity Framework Core 2.0 at `https://www.packtpub.com/product/mastering-entity-framework-core-20/9781788294133`.

In this section, we'll update a small ASP.NET application that uses Entity Framework Core with all of the standards we discussed in the previous section, with a few additional techniques to help understand Entity Framework Core even better.

Overview

In this example, we'll use our previous `DbContext` instance with `Attractions` and `Locations` tables and create a database with SQL Server.

> **Running the Web Application**
>
> The application used for this section is found on the Packt Publishing GitHub repository under `Ch5/EFApplication`.

We'll keep our data access simple. We'll use the services approach, accepting a `DbContext` instance to retrieve our data and create our database from our `DbContext` model in SQL Server.

Creating the Database

For our application to work, we need to create our database in SQL Server. Since we already have our `DbContext` instance created (using the model-first approach), we can use Entity Framework Core migrations to build our tables.

To create your local version of the database, type the following into the Package Manager Console (navigate to this via **View | Other Windows | Package Manager Console**):

```
Update-Database
```

Once you hit *Enter*, Entity Framework Core will locate the DbContext instance, read the configuration file (appsettings.json), and use the connection string to create our database and tables with seed data in it.

Adding an Asynchronous Read-Only Mode

Our first matter at hand is to apply async/await to the correct services so that we can scale the application later. If you are working with an existing ASP.NET application with Entity Framework and want to use async/await methods, it's best to start with the database. If you are creating a "greenfield" project (meaning from scratch), use async/await methods right away to save yourself headaches later.

In the AttractionService and LocationService classes, we can convert all LINQ calls as follows:

```
public List<Attraction> GetAttractions()
{
    return _context.Attractions
        .ToList();
}
```

We convert them into the following with async/await:

```
public async Task<List<Attraction>> GetAttractionsAsync()
{
    return await _context.Attractions
        .ToListAsync();
}
```

Also, since we're not creating, updating, or deleting data, we can safely say this is a read-only query. So, we can apply a .AsNoTracking() method to the query, as follows:

```
public async Task<List<Attraction>> GetAttractionsAsync()
{
    return await _context.Attractions
        .AsNoTracking()
        .ToListAsync();
}
```

As mentioned before, the .AsNoTracking() method will reduce the Entity Framework overhead since we aren't tracking the model's state but are simply populating the model.

Including Child Entities

When we query our attractions, we also want the attraction's location. How do we include the location (stored in a separate table) in our query?

As we call the GetAttractionsAsync() method, we place a .Include() method to retrieve the related entity. Our new GetAttractionsAsync() method is modified to match the following code:

```
public async Task<List<Attraction>> GetAttractionsAsync()
{
    return await _context.Attractions
        .AsNoTracking()
        .Include(r=> r.Location)
        .ToListAsync();
}
```

The .Include() method relies heavily on the database relationships you created when building your model. I'll refer you back to the "confirming your model" best practice we previously discussed. Entity Framework Core uses the model's relationships to load related entities.

Extending your Model

In our Location model, we need a way to know how many attractions are available at a location; we need a new property called AttractionCount.

While this is a simple property added to the Location class, there are multiple decisions to be made here.

First, let's create a new file under the Partials folder with the same class name, Location:

```
namespace EFApplication.DataContext.Models;

public partial class Location
{
    public int AttractionCount { get; set; }
}
```

In the preceding code snippet, something may look strange. Even though the file is located in the Partials folder, *the partial namespace has to be the same namespace as the entities' primary model* for the partial to work. .NET projects typically follow the convention of namespaces matching folder structures.

When we run our application, we should experience a problem with our `Location` model as it currently stands, as represented here:

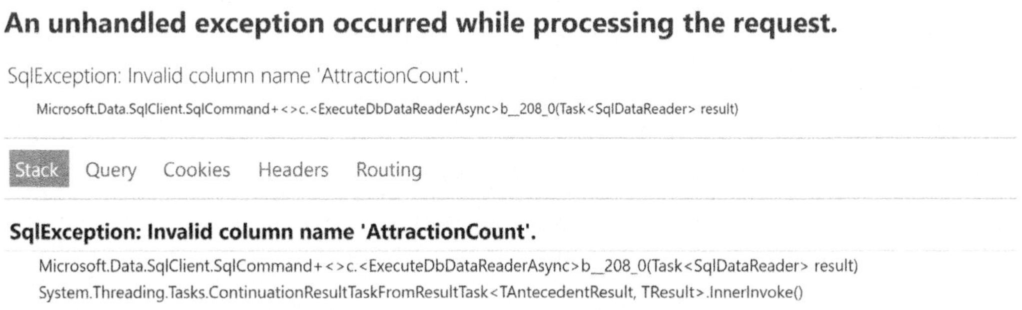

An unhandled exception occurred while processing the request.

SqlException: Invalid column name 'AttractionCount'.

Microsoft.Data.SqlClient.SqlCommand+<>c.<ExecuteDbDataReaderAsync>b__208_0(Task<SqlDataReader> result)

Stack   Query   Cookies   Headers   Routing

SqlException: Invalid column name 'AttractionCount'.

Microsoft.Data.SqlClient.SqlCommand+<>c.<ExecuteDbDataReaderAsync>b__208_0(Task<SqlDataReader> result)

System.Threading.Tasks.ContinuationResultTaskFromResultTask<TAntecedentResult, TResult>.InnerInvoke()

Figure 5.3 – The error message when you create a property on an Entity Framework object

What Entity Framework Core is telling us is there isn't an `AttractionCount` field in the table and it can't populate the property since it doesn't exist.

We have three options here, as follows:

1. Place a `[NotMapped]` attribute on the property so that it doesn't try to populate the property and count our attractions by hand.

2. Create a SQL Server function to calculate a calculated property called `AttractionCount` and return it so that it can populate our extra property.

3. Automatically count the number of attractions already in the model.

Let's focus on implementing *option 3* as a quick hit for success.

While we do need a `[NotMapped]` attribute so that Entity Framework Core doesn't try to load it, we'll change the property into an `expression-bodied` property. We could make this an auto property (`{get;set;}`), but we're only using this as a `get` property, as shown in the following code snippet:

```
public partial class Location
{
    [NotMapped]
    public int AttractionCount => Attractions.Count;
}
```

Keep in mind this is assuming you have a foreign-key relationship in your SQL Server instance created to load the attractions when a location is loaded. If you don't have a `.Include()` method, your attraction count will be 0.

In this section, we learned how to create databases using the model-first approach, how to add an asynchronous, read-only mode using the `.AsNoTracking()` method so the state isn't attached to the objects, how to include child entities when retrieving a parent model, and finally, how to extend your model using a partial class and attaching a `[NotMapped]` attribute to properties, letting Entity Framework know whether it should map a field to the property.

Summary

In this chapter, we learned about three different Entity Framework Core patterns including Repository and Unit of Work, Specification, and Extension Methods and how to implement each one into your own projects.

Then, we examined some of the standards in the industry, such as confirming your model, adding `async`/`await` to your LINQ calls, implementing logging, using resource files for seeding data, and understanding deferred execution.

We also reviewed how to perform read-only queries and how to leverage the database by letting it perform data-intensive procedures.

Finally, we applied these standards to an existing application with a way to create our database using the model-first approach, then examined how to add an asynchronous, read-only mode using the `.AsNoTracking()` method so that state isn't attached to objects, how to include child entities when retrieving a parent model, and finally, how to extend your model while letting Entity Framework know which properties to populate and which properties to ignore.

In the next chapter, we'll learn about UI standards with MVC, Razor Pages, ViewComponents, HTMLHelpers, and Task Runners.

6

Best Practices with Web User Interfaces

When creating a **user interface (UI)** with ASP.NET 8, it can be intimidating since most developers are so used to working with C#. There are a lot of factors to consider when creating a web application, such as avoiding duplication, recognizing similar interfaces for reusable components, creating a structured website, and making it easier for search engines to index the site—a process known as **search engine optimization (SEO)**.

In this chapter, we're going to cover the following main topics:

- Using a task runner
- Applying standards to UIs
- Introducing Buck's coffee shop project

In the first section, we'll examine why a task runner is so important to developers, how to set it up and run it automatically, and how to bundle and minify scripts. Then, in the next section, we'll review a number of common standards with ASP.NET 8 sites, including centralizing links, keeping controllers and Razor Pages small, why `ViewComponent` classes are better than the `HTMLHelper` class or partials, replacing HTML helpers with tag helpers, and why creating SEO-friendly URLs are important.

Finally, we'll create a new project called *Buck's Coffee Shop*, applying everything we've covered.

By the end of this chapter, we'll know how to include client-side resources into a task runner, implement common practices for UIs, understand how to build additional functionality into an existing web application using the Task Runner tool, consolidate links using extension methods, and extend HTML by creating our own HTML Tags.

Technical requirements

Even with a simple web UI, the Visual Studio family of products creates an easy way to build web applications using IntelliSense. We recommend using your favorite editor to view the GitHub repository. We recommend the following:

- Visual Studio (latest version)
- Visual Studio Code
- JetBrains Rider

The editor we'll be using is Visual Studio 2022 Enterprise, but any version (Community or Professional) will work with the code.

The code for *Chapter 6* is located in Packt Publishing's GitHub repository, found at `https://github.com/PacktPublishing/ASP.NET-Core-8-Best-Practices`.

Using a task runner

In this section, we'll explain what a task runner is, what its responsibilities are, how to automatically execute it when building the solution, and provide some examples of how to use it.

As developers, we are always looking for better ways to quickly automate tasks. With JavaScript frameworks, this task is essential, especially when building the solution in a **Continuous Integration/ Continuous Delivery (CI/CD)** pipeline. The consistent repetition of certain tasks becomes monotonous and takes away from development time. Why not have a computer process the work?

As developers, the need to include a task runner section in this chapter is meant to show developers how to automate tasks to make client-side endeavors more efficient. In recent years, I've experienced developers who've never used a task runner for client-side tasks or even know what it is. A task runner is a tremendous benefit to all developers.

What is a task runner?

As JavaScript became popular, developers wanted a way to build their JavaScript as well as build their solutions. In addition to using JavaScript, TypeScript was created to give JavaScript more of a strong-typed feel and required a compilation step as well.

Along with "compiling" TypeScript, most websites require additional tasks such as minifying and bundling JavaScript and optimizing. There was a need for a tool to make the developer's experience seamless when working with C# and JavaScript.

This is why the Task Runner tool was created and integrated into Visual Studio. Its primary responsibility is to automate tasks using either Grunt or Gulp with build scripts.

Gulp and Grunt are also task runners, but each one has a different file format in JavaScript when defining tasks. While we can use either Grunt or Gulp scripts in the Visual Studio Task Runner, we'll be using the Gulp format.

The Task Runner in Visual Studio is what I would consider a "mini-pipeline for the client side." A task runner is a great introduction for developers learning to create a CI/CD pipeline for an application.

Setting up the Task Runner

The Task Runner relies heavily on Node.js for running scripts. By default, Node.js should already be installed through Visual Studio.

To find out whether Node.js is installed on your machine, do the following:

1. Select **Package Manager Console** from **View | Other Windows**.

2. When a prompt appears, type `npm --version`. If it displays a version number, we can proceed with the next step. If not, a repair of Visual Studio through the Visual Studio Installer may be required.

3. Type `npm install -g gulp --save-dev`. The `-g` option is to install Gulp globally, and `--save-dev` is there to save the dependency in the `package.json` file. With that said, there should be a `package.json` file added to the solution.

4. Add a new JavaScript file to the root of the project, called `gulpfile.js`.

Depending on whether we're using Grunt or Gulp, the Task Runner requires a specific file. In the examples (as I mentioned before), we'll be using the Gulp format.

Structure of a gulpfile

When creating a gulpfile, it should be named `gulpfile.js`. The file should be placed into the root of the solution.

The structure of a gulpfile contains the following:

*   **Defined packages**—These are the modules used throughout the gulpfile.

*   **Processing and cleanup tasks**—Each task will contain a process task along with a cleanup task.

*   **Export groupings**—This provides a list of tasks to execute in a specific order. Usually, cleanup procedures are used first, followed by regular processing tasks.

Gulp requires a `gulpfile.js` file to be located in the root of the solution. The standard layout of a gulpfile is usually segmented using the following structure:

- **Packages defined at the top**—The packages at the top are the modules installed through your npm installs.

- **Tasks (processing and cleanup)**—For every automated concept in a `gulpfile.js` file, there should be two tasks: a processing task and a cleanup task. The processing task is meant to achieve what we want to automate, whereas the cleanup task is meant to delete created or processed files.

- **Global default and cleanup tasks**—Segment the processing and cleanup tasks into logical groupings when building the scripts.

Since we already have our file, we'll create a simple task for our solution. Copy the following JavaScript code into the new `gulpfile.js` file:

```javascript
const { series } = require('gulp');

// Packages defined at the top
const gulp = require('gulp');

// Tasks (no cleanup for Hello World) ;-)
function testTask(done) {
    console.log('Hello World! We finished a task!');
    done();
}

// Global default and cleanup tasks
exports.build = series(
    testTask
);
```

Since this is a build script, we'll be using the `series()` function from the Gulp package, which defines sequential processes. This is represented through the first line. The second line creates a `const` instance representing the Gulp package, making the Gulp functions available to us.

Our simple task for the Task Runner is the world-famous "Hello World!" task defined through the `testTask` function while passing in the `done` function, which Gulp handles for us.

Finally, we attach a `build` property to our exports that defines a series of tasks from the preceding code. The `series` function is defined in the Gulp package. The name following the `exports` namespace can be named anything which appears in the Task Runner. If the build task isn't displaying in the Task Runner, click the **Refresh** button and it should reload the `gulpfile.js` file.

When right-clicking on the **build** option (or double-click), the build will execute showing the results, as displayed in the following screenshot:

Figure 6.1 – Results from our first Task Runner process

In the next section, we'll learn how to run our gulpfile automatically when we build our solution.

Running automatically

To assist in automatically running our gulpfile.js file, we have the ability to bind certain tasks to events when building the solution. Right-click on the task in the Task Runner to select the appropriate action for the builds, as follows:

- **Before Build**—Execute a task before compiling the solution
- **After Build**—Execute a task after the solution compiled
- **Clean Build**—Execute a task on a "Clean Solution" or "Clean <Project>" action
- **Project Open**—Execute a task after the project opens

When we select **Before Build**, the following line will be added to the top of the gulpfile.js file:

```
/// <binding BeforeBuild='build' />
```

When we build the application, the Task Runner executes the build task and, if successful, it proceeds to compile the application, as shown in the following screenshot. If not, the Task Runner will display an error message in the results pane:

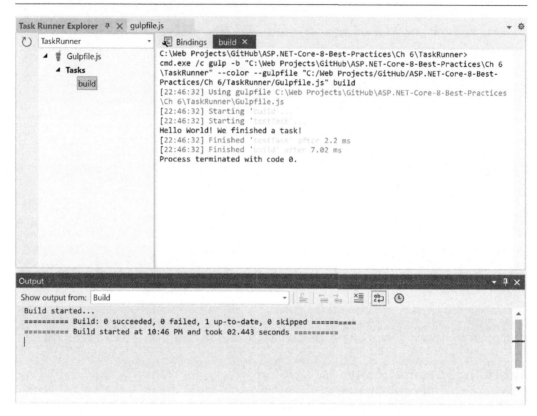

Figure 6.2 – A successful build of client-side tasks and solution

While this provides a basic foundation for our application, we need to define our client-side directory structure so that when adding resources such as images, scripts, and styles, our tasks know where to find the resources.

In the next section, we'll look at how to set up the structure for our client-side workflow.

Creating a workflow structure

Before we write scripts for our `gulpfile.js` file, we need to define a simple workflow for our Task Runner. Generally, our gulpfile contains, at the very least, a JavaScript and CSS bundler and minifier. It doesn't matter which one is executed first, but they could even be candidates for a collection of parallel tasks. While Visual Studio created our server-side application, the client-side structure requires a little more attention in regard to where to place files throughout our application.

In every ASP.NET 8 application, we have a `wwwroot` folder that contains our client-side scripts, styles, and static content (such as images). This is considered the root path to our application for our static content, so if we have a website called `https://www.mywebsite.com/, the wwwroot` folder will be our root. For example, if we want to access our CSS folder, we'd access it via `https://www.mywebsite.com/css/`. While every resource (such as scripts and styles) has its own way of processing and creating production-ready output files, there needs to be a workflow on how each task in our Task Runner will perform.

The current directory structure looks like this:

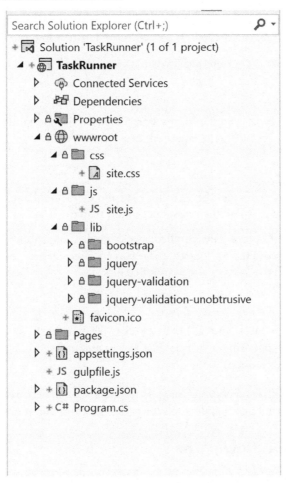

Figure 6.3 – A common ASP.NET 8 structure

The preceding structure is meant for a production-level application. The css directory doesn't contain any SASS or LESS files for processing, and the js directory has only simple JavaScript files. We need additional directories for our workflow to function properly.

For our application, we'll be using TypeScript and SASS. SASS is a preprocessor for CSS files and requires a directory for our source files (with an extension of .scss). TypeScript also requires transpilation into JavaScript files, so we'll create a scss directory for our SASS files and a src directory for our TypeScript files.

Create a src folder and a scss folder under the wwwroot folder. These folders will contain the source code for our application. The src folder will contain all TypeScript files for the application, whereas the scss folder will contain all of the styles ready for compilation into production-ready CSS files.

The following steps show a common workflow for a task runner:

1. TypeScript files:

    *   Transpile the TypeScript files in the src folder into JavaScript files. The output files will reside in the src folder. The output files are JavaScript files.

2. JavaScript files:

    *   Use a bundler to process the .js files. The bundler should automatically know how to include all files based on the JavaScript module pattern.

    *   Use a minifier to process the bundled JavaScript files. The output files are copied from the src folder over to the js folders. These files are also renamed to have a .min.js suffix added to them to identify them as minified files.

3. Styles:

    *   Use a "styler compiler" such as LESS or SASS. We'll be using SASS to precompile our styles. These files will reside in the scss folder. Once compiled, the folder will contain .css files and be inevitably moved to the css folder.

The workflow structure of our application implies the js and css folders are production-level folders while making our src and scss folders specific to developer modifications.

Defining our workflow paths

Since we created our workflow structure, we need to tell Gulp where our source and destination folders reside in our application. The path module contains a resolve function to concatenate folder names as we go, as shown here:

```
// Packages defined at the top
const gulp = require('gulp'),
```

```
       path = require('path');

// define our paths for our app
const basePath = path.resolve(__dirname, "wwwroot");
```

`__dirname` is a reserved word and is based on the current directory (in our case, this is the root of our application). `basePath` is used to operate solely in the `wwwroot` folder and below and won't interfere with our ASP.NET 8 application.

Transpiling TypeScript

Our first order of business is to transpile our TypeScript files into JavaScript files. Transpiling is the process of converting TypeScript into JavaScript. With most of our TypeScript projects, we almost always have a `tsconfig.json` configuration file, and this will reside in the root of the `wwwroot` folder. However, we need a special package for reading the configuration file specifically for Gulp.

To include the package, proceed as follows:

1. In the **Package Manager Console**, type `npm install -g gulp-cli`. It should then be added to your `package.json` file.

2. In the **Package Manager Console**, type `npm install gulp@4` to install Gulp as a project dependency.

3. One last time in the **Package Manager Console**, type `npm install gulp-typescript typescript gulp-clean --save-dev` to install TypeScript, the `gulp-typescript`, and the ability to remove files (`gulp-clean`).

4. Define the module at the top of the `gulpfile.js` file, like so:

    ```
    const gulp = require('gulp'),
          path = require('path'),
          tsConfig = require("gulp-typescript");
    ```

5. Load the configuration using the `createProject` function referencing the path to the `tsconfig.json` file, as follows:

    ```
    // define our paths for our app
    const basePath = path.resolve(__dirname, "wwwroot");
    const tsProject = tsConfig.createProject(path.resolve(basePath,
    'tsconfig.json'));
    ```

6. Define the TypeScript source folder, like so:

    ```
    const tsSource = path.resolve(basePath, "src");
    ```

7. We'll keep track of paths through a source object. Our `srcPaths` object will contain a `js` path pointing to our source code:

```
const srcPaths = {
    js: [
        path.resolve(tsSource, '**/*.js')
    ]
};
```

8. We need to create process (`ts_transpile`) and cleanup (`ts_cleanup`) functions for our TypeScript. Here's the code to achieve that:

```
function ts_transpile(done) {
    tsProject
        .src()
        .pipe(tsProject()).js
        .pipe(gulp.dest(tsSource));
    done();
}

function ts_clean(done) {
    gulp.src(srcPaths.js, {allowEmpty: true})
        .pipe(clean({ force: true }));
    done();
}
```

9. The `ts_transpile` function uses the `tsProject` configuration to locate the source files (through the `include` property near the end of the `tsconfig.json` file) and convert all of the TypeScript files into JavaScript files in the same directory.

10. Our `ts_clean` function will simply remove all JavaScript (*NOT* TypeScript) files from every directory.

11. Once we have our TypeScript tasks defined, we simply add them to our build process at the bottom of our `gulpfile.js` file, like so:

```
// Global default and cleanup tasks
exports.build = series(
    ts_clean,
    ts_transpile
);
```

12. First, we delete all of the JavaScript files with `ts_clean`, then perform the transpiling with `ts_transpile`.

13. As shown in the example, our workflow structure locates all of the TypeScript files and transpiles them into JavaScript files:

Figure 6.4 – TypeScript files in src folders converted to JavaScript

Since our TypeScript is now transpiled down to JavaScript, we can focus on bundling and minifying the files.

Bundling and minifying

By nature, JavaScript takes a while to load in the browser. To make matters worse, if a JavaScript file is formatted for readability, the file takes even longer to load, therefore making it slower to download. A minification process is necessary to shorten the loading process as much as possible to give the user a better experience.

Bundling is the concept of taking an application's scripts and styles and combining them into one script or style instead of loading multiple files.

Since spaces and tabs take up…well, space, minifying the scripts and styles is the process of shrinking client-side files down to a smaller size for faster delivery to the browser.

To bundle our scripts, we need a module called Browserify for our Gulp script. Let's start adding the bundling functionality to the `gulpfile.js` file. Here are the steps:

1. In the **Package Manager Console**, type `npm install -g browserify gulp-rename vinyl-source-stream vinyl-buffer vinyl-transform gulp-uglify-es`. We should see these modules added to the `package.json` file.

2. Once these are installed in the `package.json` file, we need to include another `srcPath` object containing all of the files we want bundled/minified:

```
const srcPaths = {
    js: [
        path.resolve(tsSource, '**/*.js') // all *.js in every
                                                        folder
    ],
    jsBundles: [
        path.resolve(tsSource, 'site.js') // specific files to
                                                        bundle/minify
    ]
};
```

We'll call the property `jsBundles`. Since every TypeScript file was transpiled into a JavaScript file, we have to identify which files to load. A good practice to follow is to name the file the same as the actual page. The good news is the Browserify module will follow the imports in each file and include it in the bundling. As we add more TypeScript to the project, add the primary script to the list for automatic compilation.

3. Create a new variable where the scripts will reside for the web application:

```
const destPaths = {
    jsFolder: path.resolve(basePath, 'js') // wwwroot/js
};
```

We'll call the variable `destPaths`.

4. Next, we create our processing and cleanup for bundling and minifying the scripts:

```
/* JavaScript */
function js_bundle_min(done) {

    srcPaths.jsBundles.forEach(file => {

        const b = browserify({
                entries: file, // Only need initial file, browserify
                                                finds the deps
```

```
                    transform: [['babelify', { 'presets': ["es2015"] }]]
            });

        b.bundle()
            .pipe(source(path.basename(file)))
            .pipe(rename(path => {
                path.basename += ".min";
                path.extname = ".js";
            }))
            .pipe(buffer())
            .pipe(uglify())
            .pipe(gulp.dest(destPaths.jsFolder));
        done();
    });
}

function js_clean(done) {
    gulp.src(path.resolve(destPaths.jsFolder, '**/*.js'), {
read: false })
        .pipe(gp_clean({ force: true }));
    done();
}
```

In the `js_bundle_min` function shown in the preceding snippet, we loop through all of the files we want bundled. We create a `browserify` object with options set and start the bundling process per file.

The first process is getting the base name of the file we're currently processing. Once we have the filename, we can rename the base from `site` to `site.min` and then add a `.js` extension to the end of the file. We then buffer the file and perform an `uglify` operation on it, meaning we minify it. After it's bundled and minified, we write the file out to the destination folder, which is `wwwroot/js`.

The `js_clean` function removes all of the `.js` files from the `wwwroot/js` folder.

5. Finally, we can add the `js_bundle_min` and `js_clean` functions to our build exports at the bottom of the file:

```
// Global default and cleanup tasks
exports.build = series(
    ts_clean,
    js_clean,
    ts_transpile,
    js_bundle_min
);
```

Once the gulpfile is saved, double-click on the build, and the files should appear in the `wwwroot/` `js` folder. If we double-click the JavaScript file, we'll see it's been bundled and minified.

Implementing additional tasks

While bundling and minifying scripts is a big deal, there are other tasks we can add to a task runner. Such tasks can include the following:

- SCSS/LESS precompiling

- Image optimization

- Release notes

- Copying `dist` folders from `node_modules` to a `lib` folder on build

These are just a few of the simple tasks available when preparing the web application. For additional tasks, refer to the source code for *Chapter 6* on GitHub in the `TaskRunner` project at `https://` `github.com/PacktPublishing/ASP.NET-Core-8-Best-Practices`.

In this section, we reviewed what a task runner is and what it can do for developers and showed how to automatically execute it when building the solution. We also demonstrated the power of the Task Runner by creating a workflow structure and defining our workflow paths, how to transpile TypeScript, and how to minify and bundle scripts. As we can see, this simplifies the developer experience by automating client-side tasks and building the solution using one build.

In the next section, we'll examine more UI standards and what is considered common knowledge when it comes to ASP.NET 8 web applications.

Applying standards to UIs

ASP.NET's web page model has evolved over the years. With Web Forms, it was `ViewState` and components. With MVC, it had partials and HTML Helpers. Now, ASP.NET 8 provides more advanced techniques using `ViewComponent` classes and `TagHelper` classes.

For this section, we'll examine how ASP.NET 8 uses its language-specific features to build quicker and more flexible UIs. We'll see how to consolidate links across a site, why it's important to keep controllers/ pages small, how `ViewComponent` classes are better than partials and `HTMLHelper` classes, and look at how to create SEO-friendly routes.

Centralizing your site links

If we have a large site with hundreds of links, developers understand what it means when a page is renamed, moved, or (gasp) deleted. It's definitely a time-consuming effort to change every link on a large site. While TagHelper classes are…well, helpful, one common practice is to use UrlHelper classes to consolidate the links.

Let's examine a website with the following ASP.NET 8 TagHelper class shown here:

```
<a asp-page="Index">Go to Main Page</a>
```

Imagine all of these on secondary pages pointing to the main page, Index.cshtml, and we receive a request to change the name of the page to Index2.

With extension methods, we can create custom site-specific UrlHelper class URLs for each page, as shown in the following example:

```
Public static class SiteLinkExtensions
{
    public static string HomeUrl(this UrlHelper helper) =>
        helper.RouteUrl(new UrlRouteContext
        {
            RouteName = "Default",
            Values = new
            {
                Controller="Home",
                Action ="Index"
            }
        });
}
```

Extension methods require three things: a static class, a static method, and the method's first parameter in the signature must have this declared.

> **What is an extension method?**
>
> For more details on using extension methods, navigate to https://learn.microsoft.com/en-us/dotnet/csharp/programming-guide/classes-and-structs/extension-methods.

We can apply this technique to Razor Pages as well using the PageLink method, as shown here:

```
Public static string DetailsUrl(this IurlHelper helper, string blogId)
=>
    helper.PageLink("Detail", values: new { Id = blogId, area =
"admin" });
```

The only difference between the two methods is the extension method attaches to an `IurlHelper` class instead of a `UrlHelper` class and, for Razor Pages, we use the `.PageLink` method instead.

If using the `TagHelper` anchor with the `asp-page` attribute, this approach limits our flexibility because we are defining a page in multiple places. By adding an extension method to the `UrlHelper` class, we can simplify it by using the HTML `href` attribute, as shown here:

```
<a href="@Url.HomeUrl()">Go to Main Page</a>
```

With `UrlHelper` extension methods, all of the links across the site are easier to integrate and more efficient to update.

Keeping controllers/pages small

When ASP.NET MVC was introduced, controllers were often the dumping ground for most code, making calls to the database, creating models, and validating the model.

MVC controllers (and now Razor Pages) should be "traffic cops," directing the logic to certain parts of the application based on the page's function.

While the following list is far from complete, certain aspects can be offloaded to other parts of ASP. NET 8 to put controllers and pages on a diet:

- **Validating models**—Instead of validating models in the controller, use data attributes such as `[Required]` and `[Email]`.

- **Database calls**—Instead of making database calls directly from the controller or Razor page, dependency inject a `DbContext` instance and use Entity Framework. If Entity Framework isn't a viable solution, offload the database processing to `Service` classes (see *Chapter 5* on Entity Framework Core).

- **Secondary processes**—If the application contains code to send emails, process records, or build an object, refactor the process out to its own class and inject it into the controller/Razor page, making it cleaner and easier to test.

Large methods in controllers or Razor Pages can complicate matters further when trying to test or debug code. Smaller code, in this instance, is the better approach.

Using ViewComponents

When HTML Helpers and Partial views were introduced with MVC, the ability to pass an object into a small section and have it create a snippet of HTML for the View was a great feature for developers. However, there were a few downsides to using these two features.

The downside of using HTML Helpers was the ability to create new HTML snippets through code and render that back to the View. If the HTML changed, it would require updating and recompiling of the code violating **separation of concerns (SoC)** ("You've got your C# in my HTML"). There wasn't any HTML associated with the Helper; it had to be created using code.

Swinging the pendulum the other way, Partials introduced the ability to have HTML with no code with the ability to pass objects into the partial. The issue with this approach was the ability to place if...then statements inside the HTML. When an if...then statement was introduced in HTML, this was considered a code smell (which is code looking like it doesn't belong or looks suspicious) and was meant to be a business rule. HTML should be declarative—almost template-like with no branching involved.

With ASP.NET Core, ViewComponent classes were introduced and, while not meant to replace HTMLHelper classes or Partials, fulfilled a larger need for building modular web applications. Considered to be "mini-controllers," ViewComponent classes provide ASP.NET developers with a better approach for the following reasons:

- **SoC**—With an HTML and C# combination, this allows a better way of writing modular components.

- **Chunky rendering**—By default, ViewComponent classes only render a chunk of the view instead of the entire response. This makes the component independently render faster.

- **Easy to test**—ViewComponent classes are isolated by nature, making them extremely easy to test. Create a new ViewComponent class, pass in arguments, and test to see if it returned what was expected.

ViewComponent classes give us the best of both worlds, rendering HTML while using C# for applying business rules in a single component.

> **Additional ViewComponent material**
>
> For more details on the ViewComponent class, navigate to https://learn.microsoft.com/en-us/aspnet/core/mvc/views/view-components.

Using Tag Helpers instead of HTML Helpers

While HTML Helpers provide the ability to create small snippets of HTML (just don't go overboard), the TagHelper class take it a step further.

The difference between Tag Helpers and HTML Helpers is TagHelper classes allow us to build our own tag elements through code and HTMLHelper classes are directly called as methods in the HTML.

For example, if we were building a hotel application, some `TagHelper` classes would include `<calendar>`, `<availability>`, and `<room-gallery>` tags. These would look like brand new tags in HTML, but ASP.NET would render them on the server and create HTML based on the data model fed to them.

Tag Helpers are an extremely powerful feature for developers wanting to create their own custom library of domain-specific HTML tags.

Creating SEO-friendly URLs

Site architecture is important when building websites. If it's a public-facing website, the site should be easy to crawl with simple URLs.

To look at this another way, examine the following two URLs:

- `https://www.mysite.com/Blog/my-first-blog-post`

- `https://www.mysite.com/?blogpost=E1FCFB35-87C7-442F-9516-7C8585E8CD49`

If we found these links and we were talking with someone on the phone, which one would we tell them to follow?

Creating friendly URLs provides the following benefits:

- **Easier to identify the page**—We know the first URL is someone's first blog post. The second URL is…well, we don't know what kind of page it is.

- **Easy to repeat**—It's easier to say the first URL over the phone as opposed to the GUID.

- **Better SEO**—If we have the opportunity, it's always good to help search engines identify what kind of page created.

> **Best practices of Google's URL structure**
>
> For better naming of URLs and what Google recommends, navigate to `https://developers.google.com/search/docs/crawling-indexing/url-structure`.

Creating these SEO-friendly URLs requires a site-wide link strategy using mapping methods such as `.MapRoute()` and, if using Razor Pages, naming pages related to the content.

In this section, we learned how to catalog our links using extension methods, how controllers and pages should be made as small as possible, how `ViewComponent` classes can improve the efforts of writing modular code, why `TagHelper` classes can propel HTML to new heights, and why creating SEO-friendly URLs is so important.

In the last section, we'll apply our knowledge of implementing these concepts into an application.

Introducing Buck's coffee shop project

We covered a lot in the last section, with various concepts explained. It's one thing to explain `ViewComponent` and `TagHelper` classes, but where do we apply these concepts on a website?

In this section, we'll apply those concepts to a brand-new project. Our friend wanted a new website for his coffee shop, so we used the ASP.NET 8 Web Application template as a starting point for the site.

Setting up Buck's website

Since we have a new website, we want to create the client-side pipeline so that we can focus on the site's functionality.

This sounds like a job for…the Task Runner.

While we've included the transpiling of TypeScript and bundling/minifying JavaScript in the project, we can add additional tasks to make our lives even easier.

One easy task is to bundle and minify our styles using SASS, as follows:

1. In the **Package Manager Console**, type `npm install --save-dev sass gulp-sass`. These modules should be added to the `package.json` file.

2. Once these are installed in the `package.json` file, we include the module as required at the top of our `gulpfile.js` file, like so:

    ```
    gp_sass = require('gulp-sass')(require("sass"));
    ```

3. Create a variable containing the path to the SCSS files:

    ```
    const sassSource = path.resolve(basePath, "scss");
    ```

4. Add the style file to the `srcPaths` object (in the `sassSrc` property):

    ```
    const srcPaths = {
        js: [
            path.resolve(tsSource, '**/*.js') // all *.js in every
                                                  folder
        ],
        jsBundles: [
            path.resolve(tsSource, 'site.js') // specific files to
                                                  bundle/minify
        ],
        sassSrc: [
    ```

```
        path.resolve(sassSource, 'site.scss')
    ]
}
```

5. Add the style path to the `destPaths` object (with the `cssFolder` property):

```
const destPaths = {
    jsFolder: path.resolve(basePath, 'js'), // wwwroot/js
    cssFolder: path.resolve(basePath, 'css') // wwwroot/css
};
```

6. Add the processing and cleaning functions:

```
/* SASS/CSS */
function sass_clean(done) {
    gulp.src(destPaths.cssFolder + "*.*", { read: false })
        .pipe(gp_clean({ force: true }));
    done();
}

function sass(done) {
    gulp.src(srcPaths.sassSrc)
        .pipe(gp_sass({ outputStyle: 'compressed' }))
        .pipe(rename({
            suffix: '.min'
        }))
        .pipe(gulp.dest(destPaths.cssFolder));
    done();
}
```

7. Finally, add the functions to the build process:

```
// Global default and cleanup tasks
exports.build = series(
    ts_clean,
    js_clean,
    sass_clean,
    ts_transpile,
    js_bundle_min,
    sass
);
```

What about those JavaScript libraries? They're in the dreaded `node_modules` folder. Most JavaScript libraries have a `dist` folder for distribution. This was the case when we installed the Bootstrap and Font Awesome libraries. Why not copy that into our `/lib` folder for our local purposes?

8. Create a variable in the `gulpfile.js` file containing the path to the `node_modules` folder. This should be in the root of the solution:

```
const moduleSource = path.resolve(__dirname, "node_modules");
```

9. Create a new variable containing the destination of where to place our `dist` packages (our `/lib` folder):

```
const libSource = path.resolve(basePath, "lib");
```

10. Define the copy details in a property called `lib`:

```
const srcPaths = {
    js: [
        path.resolve(tsSource, '**/*.js') // all *.js in every
                                          folder
    ],
    jsBundles: [
        path.resolve(tsSource, 'site.js') // specific files to
                                          bundle/minify
    ],
    sassSrc: [
        path.resolve(sassSource, 'site.scss')
    ],
    // local dev (copy dist into lib)
    lib: [
        {
            src: path.resolve(moduleSource, 'bootstrap/
                dist/**/*'),
            dest: path.resolve(libSource, 'bootstrap/')
        },
        {
            src: path.resolve(moduleSource, '@fortawesome/
                fontawesome-free/**/*'),
            dest: path.resolve(libSource, 'fontawesome/')
        }
    ]
};
```

11. Add the processing and cleaning functions:

```
/* Copy Libraries to their location */
function copyLibraries(done) {
    srcPaths.lib.forEach(item => {
        return gulp.src(item.src)
            .pipe(gulp.dest(item.dest));
    });
```

```
        done();
    }

    function cleanLibraries(done) {
        srcPaths.lib.forEach(item => {
            return gulp.src(item.dest + "/*.*")
                .pipe(gp_clean({ force: true }));
        });
        done();
    }
```

12. Finally, add our library copy to the build process:

```
// Global default and cleanup tasks
exports.build = series(
    cleanLibraries,
    copyLibraries,
    ts_clean,
    js_clean,
    sass_clean,
    ts_transpile,
    js_bundle_min,
    sass
);
```

This gives us the ability to automatically receive the latest versions of packages for our application. When updating our package.json file, we'll benefit from the latest versions in node_modules delivered right to our /lib folder.

Updating the links

Since we have a new application, we'll create Url Helpers to help catalog the site. Based on the template, we have two links: Home and Privacy. Let's create those Url Helpers, as follows:

```
public static class BucksUrlExtensions
{
    public static string HomeUrl(this IUrlHelper helper) =>
        helper.PageLink("/Index")!;

    public static string PrivacyUrl(this IUrlHelper helper) =>
        helper.PageLink("/Privacy")!;
}
```

This makes our HTML easier to read. Instead of the Anchor Tag Helpers, we can substitute them with a Url Helper. Here is the result of replacing the Privacy Anchor Tag Helper:

```
<footer class="border-top footer text-muted">
    <div class="container">
        &copy; 2023 - Buck's Coffee Shop - <a href="@Url.
PrivacyUrl()">Privacy</a>
    </div>
</footer>
```

While this is one instance on this page, we can already see the dividends of our efforts. Notice the navigation bar?

In the navigation bar, there's another location where we can remove the hardcoded URL and use a strongly typed UrlHelper class, as illustrated here:

```
<ul class="navbar-nav flex-grow-1">
    <li class="nav-item">
        <a class="nav-link text-dark" href="@Url.HomeUrl()">Home</a>
    </li>
    <li class="nav-item">
        <a class="nav-link text-dark" href="@Url.
PrivacyUrl()">Privacy</a>
    </li>
</ul>
```

There are Privacy and Home links we replaced.

The technique also works with controllers or Razor Pages. If we need to redirect to another page, there is a UrlHelper class available to us by default, as shown here:

```
public IActionResult OnGet()
{
    return Redirect(Url.HomeUrl());
}
```

It removes the need for hardcoded URLs, providing a more efficient way of referencing links across a large website.

Creating an OffCanvas Tag Helper

Since responsive websites are important, we need to have an OffCanvas menu for when users see the site with a mobile device.

OffCanvas menus are activated on mobile devices when clicking on a hamburger menu (shown as three lines on top of each other). OffCanvas menus are hidden from the main content on a web page, hence the name. They're only necessary to hide navigational items until they're actually needed.

We're creating an OffCanvas menu for Buck's website. However, we want to use this on multiple sites, so there is a requirement to create a reusable component.

Bootstrap has an OffCanvas component and, while it's simple HTML, we can turn this into a reusable component with Tag Helpers.

First, we need the structure of a Tag Helper. Here's the code we need to execute:

```
[HtmlTargetElement("offcanvas")]
public class OffCanvasTagHelper: TagHelper
{
    [HtmlAttributeName("id")]
    public string Id { get; set; }

    [HtmlAttributeName("tabindex")]
    public string TabIndex { get; set; }

    public override async Task ProcessAsync(TagHelperContext context,
        TagHelperOutput output)
    {
        var childData = (await output.GetChildContentAsync()).
GetContent();

        output.Attributes.Clear();
        output.TagName = "div";
        output.Attributes.Add("class", "offcanvas offcanvas-start");

        if (!string.IsNullOrEmpty(Id))
        {
            output.Attributes.Add("id ", Id);
        }

        if (!string.IsNullOrEmpty(TabIndex))
        {
            output.Attributes.Add("tabindex", TabIndex);
        }
```

```
            output.Content.SetHtmlContent(childData);
    }
}
```

At the beginning of the code, we need to identify which HTML Tag we want to use for our Tag Helper. In this case, it's a simple offcanvas tag. Since HTML tags, attributes, and CSS classes are all lowercase by default, every reference to the OffCanvas class should contain a lowercase string of the tag.

We want to include an ID and a tab index based on the examples, so we need two properties called Id and TabIndex, with [HtmlAttributeName] data annotations applied to each property.

The primary method is the ProcessAsync (or Process) method. We immediately grab any children inside the offcanvas tag and process the child tags, which we'll get to later in this section.

We set tagname to DIV, set classname to offcanvas, set the attributes, and finally, set innerHTML to the child data retrieved from the beginning of the ProcessAsync method.

According to the Bootstrap OffCanvas documentation, we need a header and a body. We can easily duplicate this code to create a header and body tag for offcanvasTagHelper:

```
[HtmlTargetElement("header", ParentTag = "offcanvas")]
public class OffCanvasHeaderTagHelper: TagHelper
{
    public override async Task ProcessAsync(TagHelperContext context,
        TagHelperOutput output)
    {
        var childData = (await output.GetChildContentAsync()).
GetContent();

        output.TagName = "div";
        output.Attributes.Add("class", "offcanvas-header");

        var header = new TagBuilder("h5")
        {
            TagRenderMode = TagRenderMode.Normal
        };
        header.Attributes.Add("id", "offcanvasLabel");
        header.AddCssClass("offcanvas-title");
        header.InnerHtml.Append(childData);

        var button = new TagBuilder("button")
        {
            TagRenderMode = TagRenderMode.Normal
        };
        button.AddCssClass("btn-close");
```

```
        button.Attributes.Add("type","button");
        button.Attributes.Add("data-bs-dismiss","offcanvas");
        button.Attributes.Add("aria-label","Close");

        output.Content.AppendHtml(header);
        output.Content.AppendHtml(button);
    }
}
```

The HTMLTargetElement data annotation is a little bit different. We called this tag header. Won't this interfere with the regular HTML header tag? Not so long as we include ParentTag as a second parameter, saying this element is only valid within an offcanvas element.

In this Process method, we create a header and button and append the HTML to the output's content at the bottom. This content is sent back to the parent offcanvasTagHelper instance as the child data.

We only need to create the body with OffCanvasBodyTagHelper, as shown in the following code:

```
[HtmlTargetElement("body", ParentTag = "offcanvas")]
public class OffCanvasBodyTagHelper: TagHelper
{
    public override async Task ProcessAsync(TagHelperContext context,
        TagHelperOutput output)
    {
        var childData = (await output.GetChildContentAsync()).
            GetContent();

        output.TagName = "div";
        output.Attributes.Add("class", "offcanvas-body");

        output.Content.SetHtmlContent(childData);
    }
}
```

This will contain the same HTMLTargetElement data annotation as our header, but we'll call this the body tag. Again, it won't interfere with the standard body HTML tag since we're inside an <offcanvas> element. We get the child data (which should be a lot of HTML), we set the class and the TagName property, and finally set the content to what was inside the body tag.

One last thing required for our tag helper to work is to include all TagHelper instances in the project through the _ViewImports.cshtml file, like so:

```
@addTagHelper *, BucksCoffeeShop
```

We can add a button to our HTML to trigger offcanvas, like so:

```
<button class="btn btn-primary btn-sm" type="button" data-bs-
toggle="offcanvas" data-bs-target="#offcanvasExample" aria-
controls="offcanvasExample">
    Open
</button>
```

We can now create a simple offcanvas component in our HTML, as shown here:

```
<offcanvas id="offcanvasExample" tabindex="-1">
    <header>Buck's Coffee Shop</header>
    <body>
        <p>
            Content for the offcanvas goes here.
            You can place just about any Bootstrap
            component or custom elements here.
        </p>
    </body>
</offcanvas>
```

Once this is rendered, it will produce the Bootstrap result of an OffCanvas component with valid HTML.

This powerful technique can be applied to create a simplified HTML language for any domain where even non-developers can understand web pages.

In this section, we took a sample website and optimized our client-side scripts and styles, centralized our links by creating URL Helper extension methods, and finally, built an OffCanvas Tag Helper to showcase how we can create our own HTML library of powerful elements.

Summary

In this chapter, we began with how important a task runner is for client-side tasks and how to set up a task runner, then understood the structure of a gulpfile and how to create a workflow structure. Once we had our task runner working, we put it to work by focusing on transpiling TypeScript into JavaScript and bundling and minifying it into something for a production website.

We proceeded with looking at what's considered a standard in the industry when it comes to UIs in ASP.NET 8. We learned about how to save time by centralizing all links in one place, why it's important to keep controllers and Razor Pages small, and the key reasons why ViewComponent classes should be used. We learned why TagHelper classes are better than HTMLHelper classes and why a site should use SEO-friendly URLs.

To finalize this chapter, we looked at an example website and had a task runner bundle and minify our styles along with updating libraries automatically on build. We also applied URL Helper extension methods to the site, making it easier to change site-wide links. Finally, we took a Bootstrap `offcanvas` HTML component and converted it into a reusable `TagHelper` class to showcase the power of Tag Helpers.

In the next chapter, we'll look at the different types of testing and what are the best ways to unit test our code.

7

Testing Your Code

Testing code is an overloaded term when it comes to development. It can refer to several concepts, such as load testing, unit tests, or integration testing, just to name a few. All testing concepts are important for developers to understand regarding the **Software Development Life Cycle** (**SDLC**). Each has its purpose and is equally important to provide stability and confidence, and even provide documentation.

In this chapter, we're going to cover the following main topics:

- Understanding testing concepts
- Best approaches for testing
- Testing Entity Framework Core

In the first section, we'll cover the basic concepts of testing, including unit, integration, regression, load, system, and UI tests.

Next, we'll review some best approaches when writing solid tests for software, including why tests are necessary, how many unit tests are required, using the **Arrange, Act, Assert** (**AAA**) technique when writing unit tests, why unit test scaffolding should be avoided, why to avoid large unit tests, how and why to avoid static methods, and, finally, how to use tests for documentation.

Finally, we'll apply our knowledge of this chapter by creating a full integration test using Entity Framework Core.

Technical requirements

We recommend using a favorite editor to view this book's GitHub repository. Our recommendations include the following:

- Visual Studio (preferably 2022, though any version is fine)
- Visual Studio Code
- JetBrains Rider

The editor we'll be using is Visual Studio 2022 Enterprise, but any version (Community or Professional) will work with the code.

The code for this chapter is located in Packt Publishing's GitHub repository, which is located in the `Chapter07` folder, at `https://github.com/PacktPublishing/ASP.NET-Core-8-Best-Practices`.

Understand testing concepts

Unit tests are important to developers because they provide stability to software, confidence in their code, and the added benefit of documenting complex code. Unit tests provide numerous benefits, as we'll see in this chapter.

In this section, we'll review the concepts of testing and why each one is important to the stability and confidence in building a website.

Unit tests

The smallest test we can write to confirm the code functions as expected is a unit test. Unit tests are usually created to test small(-ish) methods, as well as to test multiple parameters sent into those methods and expect a certain result.

Identifying the types of unit tests to write is a simple process of finding conditions in a method and writing the relevant test for the behavior.

The following scenarios could justify unit tests throughout a method:

- Successful flow of a method (that is, the happy path)
- Failure of a method's behavior (that is, the unhappy path)
- Any branching or condition (if..then, switch, inline if, and so on)
- Different parameters passed into the method
- Exception handling

If we have a large system, the number of unit tests is expected to be in the hundreds since these small, granular methods comprise most of the system.

The following example shows an extension method formatting a date/time object for display purposes. Since it's self-contained, we can simply create a date/time object and test it:

```
[TestMethod]
public void FormattedDateTimeWithTimeTest()
{
    // Arrange
    var startDate = new DateTime(2023, 5, 2, 14, 0, 0);
```

```
    const string expected = @"May 2<sup>nd</sup>, 2023 at 2:00pm";

    // Act
    var actual = startDate.ToFormattedDateTime();

    // Assert
    Assert.AreEqual(expected, actual);
}
```

This code creates a new date with a time. The unit test is formatted using the AAA technique (which we'll cover in a bit) and returns a string to be displayed in our HTML.

Once unit tests are in place, the next step is to provide integration tests.

Integration tests

The next level of testing is integration tests, which require additional functionality as to how the system is tested. Integration tests involve grouping modules and the ability to test those components as a group, which contrasts with unit tests.

In my experience, the primary difference between integration and unit tests is external resources. If a unit test accesses an external resource (such as a disk drive, database, network call, or API), it can be considered an integration test.

The following example shows a simple integration test where we're connecting to a local test database to confirm the connection of the database and returning a valid IndexModel object:

```
[TestClass]
public class PageTests
{
    private DbContextOptions<ThemeParkDbContext> _options;
    private ThemeParkDbContext _context;

    [TestInitialize]
    public void Setup()
    {
        _options = new DbContextOptionsBuilder<ThemeParkDbContext>()
            .UseSqlServer("Data Source=localhost;Initial
                Catalog=ASPNetCore8BestPractices;" +
                "Integrated
                Security=True;MultipleActiveResultSets=True;")
                .Options;

        var config = new Mock<IConfiguration>();
```

```
        _context = new ThemeParkDbContext(_options, config.Object);
    }

    [TestMethod]
    [TestCategory("Integration")]
    public void ReturnAnIndexModelTest()
    {
        // Arrange
        var logger = new Mock<ILogger<IndexModel>>();
        var service = new AttractionService(_context);

        // Act
        var actual = new IndexModel(logger.Object, service);

        // Assert
        Assert.IsNotNull(actual);
        Assert.IsInstanceOfType(actual, typeof(IndexModel));
    }
}
```

In `DbContextOptionsBuilder`, we created a connection to our local database, created a valid `AttractionService` while passing in our valid `ThemeParkDbContext`, and confirmed we have the right type of model.

In the end, there are different ways to conduct integration tests, such as creating a mocked-up database or API, duplicating an environment, or even creating a new server for our tests.

Regression tests

Regression tests are the functional and nonfunctional tests we've performed in the past. By nature, these are the past successful tests we ran against the system. Regression tests are types of tests that are conducted to confirm new features don't break existing features. These include the unit tests and integration tests.

Load testing

Once you have the tests (unit and integration) running in the CI/CD pipeline (see *Chapter 2*) and are expecting a large number of users to hit the site, it is advantageous to create load test(s) for the site.

When load testing a website, subject it to stress levels beyond what a single developer experiences when running the site standalone. Load testing simulates a large number of users hitting the website concurrently and reports on whether the site can handle a large influx of users.

The results of a load test may require several team members to help with the performance of the website. Not only would developers be involved, but **database administrators** (**DBAs**), system administrators, and even architects would be involved with fixing the performance of the site.

A continuous increase in performance should be the goal of the website and creating load tests to measure performance is key to that.

System testing (end-to-end or E2E)

System testing is based on certain scenarios and is a team effort. Users of the system test new features introduced into the system while other team members conduct regression system testing to confirm new features don't break existing features.

Members of the team create scenarios for users. These users are then asked to walk through each scenario and provide feedback on whether it works or not.

One example scenario could be broken down into several categories, as shown here:

- Shopping cart:

  - Log in to the website

  - Place an item into the shopping cart

  - Click on checkout

  - Receive a confirmation page with an order number

If the scenario succeeds, the top scenario ("shopping cart") will contain a green checkmark, meaning all steps passed with no issues. If one of the steps failed, a red "X" with a reason underneath it would appear and be placed into the backlog for developers to examine later.

These types of tests require multiple users to go through the site and find issues with certain scenarios. There are times when manually testing a site is necessary, but if there's time available, it may make sense to automate these scenarios using a **user interface** (**UI**) testing approach.

UI testing

UI testing is visually conducted through a software tool such as Selenium or Cypress and automates an end user clicking around or a customer navigating the website based on a given scenario. This requires a tester to understand how the UI testing software works; they should know how to access elements on a page, know how to place values into those elements, and know how to activate events such as click and blur to simulate an end user clicking a button.

These types of tests are usually done after work hours through a CI/CD pipeline but can be run during work hours on a dedicated server (that is, a QA server) to identify issues early.

In this section, we reviewed various types of testing, including unit tests, integration tests, regression tests, load tests, system tests, and UI testing, and how each one is important and leverages the other.

In the next section, we'll look at what developers are accustomed to when it comes to unit tests, including why we write unit tests, debunking the 100% test coverage myth, how using AAA is a great approach for unit tests, why we should write a unit test library, creating large unit tests, why unnecessary mocks should be avoided, and why unit tests have the added benefit of documentation. We'll also learn how to identify slow integration tests, when to write a unit test, and how to avoid testing .NET code.

Best approaches for testing

Every company has its way of testing software. Whether it's manually or automated, it's a requirement for developers. Developers are becoming more than just people who type code. We're required to design, write, test, debug, document, build, and deploy software.

Automating tests using a CI/CD approach is where companies can save time and provide consistent stability and quality when releasing software to the public.

In this section, we'll cover the standards of why testing is important, how to avoid the 100% test coverage myth, what AAA is and why it's a great approach for unit tests, how to avoid writing a unit test library, large unit tests, and unnecessary mocks. We'll also learn about why tests have the added benefit of documentation, how to identify slow integration tests, when to write a unit test, and how to avoid testing .NET code.

Why do we write tests?

While some believe testing starts with developers, I believe it should start with management.

Developers consider tests as an absolute requirement when writing software, but if management believes tests are a waste of time, it may be time to update the resume.

Management, and possibly some developers, have various opinions about the stability of their software and the impact tests have on timetables.

The reason for tests is simple: it allows developers to confirm the code they write to perform as expected. Further, if tests are providing a simple way to consume a certain module of code, those tests provide clarity to others as well as the original author, for that matter.

The "100% test coverage" myth

As we swing the pendulum to the other side, some managers require 100% test coverage. While some people believe it's possible, 100% is not achievable or desirable.

Tests should be created where they are needed, not just for the sake of coverage. This creates a false metric and presents an illusion of "100% test coverage" if some unit tests are included to fulfill a metric. Developers may build tests just to "make their quota" to achieve this mythical metric. Each test should provide integrity with solid results and value.

This metric goes hand in hand with the **Line-Of-Code** (**LoC**) false metric as well because a developer who can write code with the least amount of lines is more efficient than a developer who writes less efficient code. More doesn't always mean better.

Using AAA

When we write our unit tests, the best way is to use the AAA technique:

- **Arrange**: Initialize the code for a test
- **Act**: Perform the actual test
- **Assert**: Determine whether the result is the expected behavior

The Arrange step should initialize the code and be as minimal as possible.

The Act step should execute the code in question and should look similar to (if not exactly) like code in production.

Finally, the Assert step compares the result with what we're expecting back from the code.

The AAA technique provides the easiest way to identify how tests in a system are tested.

Avoid writing unit test code for your code

While the AAA concept is a simple way of writing unit tests, there is another approach that I consider a code smell.

Imagine this scenario: the developer has to write a unit test where they have to make a database call using Entity Framework Core. The Arrange step has 30 lines of code to prepare the Act step to work properly. The developer takes these 30 lines of code and moves them into a library, making them available for other unit tests.

These 30 lines of code are the code smell I mentioned. It makes more sense to refactor the code and abstract it even further to simplify the code. The Arrange step should not include an additional library of custom code to run a unit test. It should focus on testing the production code already written, not writing additional testing code to make the code pass.

However, if there is a need for a helper library, it shouldn't contain any branching statements, which would require the need to unit test the unit testing helper library.

Avoid large unit tests

Developers have various definitions of what "large" is considered. Unit tests with more than one page (a screen) of code or more than 30 lines of code should be avoided.

These types of unit test methods present a problem: they are one step away from creating a library for the Arrange step from our previous tip.

Again, it's considered a code smell, where someone may need to take a step back and look at better ways to produce smaller setups instead of large code blocks of initialization.

Avoid unnecessary mocks, fakes, or stubs

There are times when a method on a class doesn't have any dependencies and is completely isolated. When we encounter this, we may not need to create a mocked object to fully unit test the method.

Mocking is when we want to test a predefined behavior where stubs return a predefined value. Fakes are fully populated objects with working implementations.

At the very beginning of this chapter, we mentioned what a unit test was. We also created a simple extension method called `.ToFormattedDateTime()`. Since it's an isolated method, we don't require a mocked date/time object. We simply call the method.

For example, if we have a large library of extension methods that contain strings, we can create a unit test, create a string, pass it in, and check the return value is what is expected. If it requires further testing, rinse and repeat with different parameters.

When there's a simple method, sometimes, it's easier to test its functionality. No mock, fake, or stub is necessary.

Using tests as documentation

Every unit test should contain some explanation of what is tested either in the method signature or in a comment explaining the situation.

Unit tests should be informative to peers (and our future self) and indicate knowledge of what's involved in the effort (or abstraction) of completing each unit test and how it relates to the production code under test.

Along with informative unit tests, directory structure can also act as documentation and can go a long way. We should mirror the directory structure of the application in the unit tests.

If we see a folder in the application (or have a project) named `Data`, create a similar folder or project for the unit tests called `Data.Tests`. While this may be a simple concept, it helps our peers know immediately where and what the tests relate to in the project.

For example, if we look at a sample project with unit tests, you may have seen this type of structure:

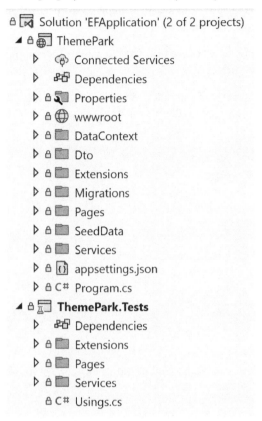

Figure 7.1 – Example of well-structured tests for a project

While some folders are missing in the ThemePark.Tests project, we can immediately see that the Extensions, Pages, and Services folders contain at least one type of test. The presence of test folders mirroring the project folders itself makes it known that they contain unit or integration tests and shows a need for additional tests to be included in the testing project.

Identifying slow integration tests

Integration tests are performed using external resources such as a database, filesystem, or API. Therefore, integration tests will always run slower than unit tests.

If we are working with a test environment to mimic another environment (such as arranging a QA environment to mimic production), the ability to detect slow connections provides a safeguard that an environment is working as expected. Ever heard the statement "It works in QA, but not in production" before?

However, if we're working with an in-memory representation of an environment, it doesn't make sense to identify whether a test is slow or not, does it? Compared to an actual environment, an in-memory representation of an environment will always run faster.

One example of this is using the Stopwatch class to gauge processes (a page or API) to determine whether they're fast or *very* fast.

If we look at our Entity Framework example from *Chapter 5*, and we add an integration test to the project, we can create a simple way to identify whether our page call is slow or not, as shown in the following example:

```csharp
using System.Diagnostics;
using EFApplication.Pages;
using EFApplication.Services;
using Microsoft.Extensions.Logging;
using Moq;

namespace ThemePark.Tests.Pages;

[TestClass]
public class PagesTest
{
    [TestMethod]
    [TestCategory("Integration")]
    public void ConfirmTheMainPageReturnsWithinThreeSecondTest()
    {
        // Arrange
        var logger = new Mock<ILogger<IndexModel>>();
        var service = new Mock<IAttractionService>();

        var stopwatch = Stopwatch.StartNew();

        // Act
        _ = new IndexModel(logger.Object, service.Object);

        // Assert
        // Make sure our call is less than 3 seconds
        stopwatch.Stop();
        var duration = stopwatch.Elapsed.Seconds;

        Assert.IsTrue(duration <= 3);
    }
}
```

In this integration test, we are testing the main page of our `ThemePark` application and finding out if it performs well or not. First, we arrange our classes, since `IndexModel` accepts `ILogger<PageModel>` and `IAttractionService`. Once we create our stopwatch, we call `IndexModel` (Act) and stop the stopwatch immediately. We convert it into seconds and conduct our Assert step.

Of course, we are performing an in-memory integration test for illustration purposes, but this concept is best suited to integration tests with external resources to identify latency issues.

In the example above, we can't tell if it's in memory or not just by reading the test. It's encapsulated in `IndexModel` and its goal is meant to identify whether it performs quick or not.

Find a bug, write a test

Unit tests are vital to a stable product, regardless of whether it's a web application or a smartphone app. Every developer will most definitely experience bugs in the application, so it makes sense to always keep the unit tests up to date.

When we (or the users) encounter a bug, repeat this mantra: *Find a bug, write a test*. This may be a simple concept, but it's recommended.

When anyone finds a bug in the application, immediately write a unit test about that bug. This gives us peace of mind when deploying an application. If we had a bug and confirmed a unit test fixed the problem, we'll have enough confidence to say it was tested before being deployed. It's one thing to fix the problem, but adding a test makes the code more bulletproof and provides confidence that the bug won't happen again.

Avoid testing .NET

.NET is a large framework. Unit tests are meant to test specific code. *YOUR code*. There is no need to create unit tests for .NET code (or other libraries/frameworks for that matter) when it's already been tested by Microsoft.

For example, if there is a test for determining whether a substring method returns the right value, this is testing the .NET framework. *Don't write this unit test*.

Our efforts are better suited to a higher scope of the method. Focus on unit testing the calling method where our code lives as opposed to a .NET method.

In this section, we examined why creating unit tests is important and why 100% test coverage is a myth. We also learned about various common unit testing strategies, such as how to use an AAA scaffolding for our unit tests, why it's considered a code smell to write additional unit test libraries when creating large unit tests, and why sometimes mocking libraries aren't necessary for everything.

We also learned about using tests as documentation using comments and folders, identifying slow integration tests by adding stopwatches, finding a bug and immediately writing a test to bulletproof our code even further, and how to avoid testing .NET methods.

In the next section, we'll review our strategies and apply them to our `ThemePark` application from *Chapter 5*.

Testing data access

Over the years, Entity Framework has strived to become unit testable and gives developers a better level of confidence when working with data access.

Building on when we created a sample database with Entity Framework Core in *Chapter 5*, in this section, we'll cover a simple way to use a SQLite in-memory database to confirm the functionality of our application… even though we don't have a database connection. Using the in-memory provider option, Microsoft has recommended avoiding this approach and using either SQLite to conduct database calls or using a production (or better, a QA) database for our queries.

> **Avoid in-memory providers**
>
> Since in-memory is an extremely simplistic implementation of a database, Microsoft has recommended using alternative methods for testing and avoiding the in-memory provider for databases. Refer to the following URL for additional details: `https://learn.microsoft.com/en-us/ef/core/testing/testing-without-the-database`.

Adding the SQLite provider

Since we don't have a way to access data yet in our tests, we have to add SQLite to get as close to an implementation as possible. Using NuGet, we have to add the following NuGet packages:

- `Microsoft.EntityFrameworkCore.Sqlite`
- `Microsoft.EntityFrameworkCore.InMemory`

Once we have those in our tests, we can proceed with creating our `AttractionService` and `LocationService` tests to confirm they work as expected.

Creating the AttractionService test

Since we are using `AttractionService` as a "repository," we only need to pass in `DbContext` for it to work as expected. Currently, `ThemeParkDbContext` creates seeded data for an empty database.

This is perfect for our needs because when passing in `ThemeParkDbContext`, `DbContext` could be an in-memory representation or an actual connection to a production database. In this case, we are creating an in-memory SQLite database for our purposes.

The SQLite provider opens connections when a call is made and deletes the connection when it's closed. We create the connection during setup and provide a [Cleanup] attribute to deallocate the connection. This is specifically for SQLite.

Our AttractionService integration test is shown in the following example:

```
using Microsoft.EntityFrameworkCore;
using System.Data.Common;
using Microsoft.Data.Sqlite;
using Microsoft.Extensions.Configuration;
using Moq;
using ThemePark.DataContext;
using ThemePark.Services;

namespace ThemePark.Tests.Services;

[TestClass]
public class AttractionServiceTest
{
    private DbConnection _connection = null!;
    private DbContextOptions<ThemeParkDbContext> _options = null!;
    private IThemeParkDbContext _context = null!;

    [TestInitialize]
    public void Setup()
    {
        _connection = new SqliteConnection("Filename=:memory:");
        _connection.Open();

        // These options will be used by the context instances in this
            test suite,
        // including the connection opened above.
        _options = new DbContextOptionsBuilder<ThemeParkDbContext>()
            .UseSqlite(_connection)
            .Options;

        var config = new Mock<IConfiguration>();

        // Create the schema and seed some data
        _context = new ThemeParkDbContext(_options, config.Object);
        _context?.Database.EnsureCreated();
    }

    [TestCleanup]
```

```
        public void Cleanup()
        {
            _connection.Dispose();
        }


        [TestMethod]
        public async Task ReturnAllAttractionsTest()
        {
            // Arrange
            var service = new AttractionService(_context);

            // Act
            var records = await service.GetAttractionsAsync();

            // Assert
            Assert.IsTrue(records.Any());
        }
    }
```

In the preceding example, we tell our tests to run the setup method using the [TestInitialize] attribute and clean up our mess using the [TestCleanup] attribute. The [TestInitialize] attribute attaches to a method for initialization purposes. The [TestCleanup] attribute identifies a method to clean up what was initialized with the [TestInitialize] attribute.

Since we're using SQLite for our database, we must create a connection in the Setup() method and open the connection. Once we open it, we need to create DbContextOptions for our fake database. The final step is to ensure the databases were created for our tests.

There are two things to notice here. The first is that we didn't need a mocked object for DbContext. In the OnConfiguring() configuration method of DbContext, if we have a configuration (such as an appsettings.json file), we should use it. If not, we should create a SQLite in-memory database for our testing.

The second thing to notice is our Act step in our integration test. This line should be the same one that we have in our production code. The closer we can get test calls to match what you have in production, the more confident we'll feel about the code, along with the accuracy and value of those tests.

Creating the LocationService test

Since we have a structure of what our tests consist of now, we can use those tests for `LocationService`. Our `LocationService` test consists of two methods – `GetAllLocationsAsync()` and `GetLocationAsync(int)`:

```
[TestMethod]
public async Task ReturnAllLocationsTest()
{
    // Arrange
    var service = new LocationService(_context);

    // Act
    var records = await service.GetLocationsAsync();

    // Assert
    Assert.IsTrue(records.Any());
}

[TestMethod]
[TestCategory("Integration")]
public async Task ReturnOneLocationByIdTest()
{
    // Arrange
    var service = new LocationService(_context);

    // Act
    var record = await service.GetLocationAsync(1);

    // Assert
    Assert.IsNotNull(record);
    Assert.IsTrue(record.Id==1);
}
```

Again, notice that we didn't need to mock `DbContext`. We created `LocationService` by passing in `ThemeParkDbContext` and used it as we would in a production environment. The ability to set up and tear down a full database is one of the greatest ways to test the database's functionality. While using an existing database would be as equally beneficial, this provides a quicker way of "setting up" and "tearing down" database functionality without the clutter or modifications when others update the database. If others are using an existing database, this could cause integration tests to fail in a CI/CD pipeline.

In this section, we learned how to set up tests with SQLite and how to perform queries using an in-memory database to mimic a production database. We also gave three examples of testing Entity Framework Core.

Summary

Testing and documentation are often areas that get deprioritized or overlooked by development teams. However, testing is a requirement for code bases. As a final point, developers should make their tests as small and fast as possible using as close to production code in the Act step as possible.

In this chapter, we covered the different types of testing, which include unit, integration, regression, load testing, system (or E2E tests), and UI testing.

Once we understood the difference between these types of testing, we examined why creating unit tests is important and why test coverage goals shouldn't be 100%. We then covered common unit testing strategies, such as how to use AAA scaffolding for our unit tests, why writing too much code for our unit tests is considered a code smell, and why mocking libraries aren't required.

Finally, we learned how to supplement documentation by using comments and folders, how to identify slow integration tests by adding stopwatches, how to find a bug and immediately write a test to bulletproof our code even further, and how to avoid testing .NET methods.

In the next chapter, we'll cover exception handling and some of the better ways to handle errors in the application.

8

Catching Exceptions with Exception Handling

We always try to make our code as stable as possible when building web applications, but there are times when we can't catch everything. This is why exceptions are considered a foundational part of development. Exception handling is essential for preventing web applications from crashing and displaying an ugly error message on a page. It's tempting to wrap everything with `try/catch` or `try/finally` statements and move on. This should be avoided. Coding with `try/catch/finally` statements in an application should be the exception to the rule.

The common coding standards in this chapter are meant to remove those types of scenarios and provide a better developer experience.

In this chapter, we'll examine what exception handling means to developers and when to use it, along with where to handle global exceptions and examine performance considerations. Once we understand the basics of exception handling, the last section will cover some common practices of exception handling, such as applying the "prevention before exception" principle to code, using logging, learning how exception handling is similar to unit tests, and why empty catch blocks should be avoided.

Finally, we'll learn how to use .NET's new exception filter, along with pattern matching, when to use `finally` blocks, and why it's a good idea to rethrow exceptions.

In this chapter, we'll cover the following main topics:

- Using exception handling
- Handling global exceptions
- Performance considerations
- Common exception handling techniques

After completing this chapter, you'll understand exception handling better, when and how to use it, how to implement global exception handling, and how to know if performance is a problem when using exception handling.

Technical requirements

We recommend using a favorite editor to add the exception handling code snippets throughout this chapter. Our recommendations are as follows:

- Visual Studio (preferably the latest version)
- Visual Studio Code
- JetBrains Rider

The editor we'll be using is Visual Studio 2022 Enterprise, but any version (Community or Professional) will work with the code.

Using exception handling

In this section, we'll discuss what exception handling is, the two types of error handling, when to use error handling in an application, and how exceptions affect performance.

What is exception handling?

Exception handling is the ability to recover gracefully from unexpected situations in the code during runtime; how do we handle errors or problems we experience in applications? It also involves cleaning up allocated resources when issues occur to avoid memory leaks.

There are two types of errors:

- **Runtime errors**: These are unexpected errors we experience when running the application.
- **Manual**: These are intentional errors that are thrown based on a condition (for instance, `ArgumentNullException.ThrowIfNull()` at the beginning of a method to confirm whether a parameter is null or not).

Since this book focuses on intermediate to advanced developers, we're assuming debugging an ASP. NET application is a common process; we all know debugging and exception handling go hand-in-hand. Developers should have a general understanding of what the code in question does when they wrap it with a `try/catch` block. The ability to create useful exceptions is extremely important. Exceptions should be clear and simple.

For example, early in my career, a developer was experiencing an error message telling them they were running out of disk space. Other developers were experiencing the same error in the application as well and were frantically trying to figure out the problem. The issue turned out to be a bad error message created by a developer along with a *server* running out of disk space, not individual developer machines. This could've been avoided by creating better log messages or detecting whether there was disk space available. While we can write better error messages in the exception handlers, we can only protect the code from so much.

Seriously, though – the ability to create a simple and clear error message can be a challenge while coding, but it does make a difference in the long run. We'll cover some of the common exception handling techniques in the next section.

When to use exception handling

The ability to identify whether or not code requires an exception handler can be tricky. In addition to whether a `try/catch/finally` block is required, are there resources involved that we need to clean up?

Context is important when it comes to exception handling. In my experience, I always ask three questions before adding exception handling:

1. **Can I legitimately handle this error myself?** An example could be using `TryParse` instead of a full `try/catch/finally` block or having to manually throw an error because of an invalid parameter.

2. **Will an external resource throw exceptions?** Examples include web APIs, storage issues, file missing, and so on.

3. **Do I have to clean up after myself if an error occurs?** Examples include losing a file connection, loading a bitmap, or a database connection.

Developers should only use exception handling when they encounter a line of code that they cannot handle and is considered outside of their control, similar to the possibility of not enough disk drive space.

In this section, we reviewed what exception handling was and when to use it properly.

Handling global exceptions

As mentioned earlier in this chapter, we can only handle so many errors when it comes to web applications. But what if we want to provide a catch-all for all unhandled exceptions?

For global exceptions, we need to revisit the middleware. There is a method called UseExceptionHandler() in the Startup.cs file that points to a /Error page (either Razor or MVC), as shown in the following code snippet:

```
if (env.IsDevelopment())
{
    app.UseDeveloperExceptionPage();
}
else
{
    app.UseExceptionHandler("/Error");
    app.UseHsts();
}
```

Pay particular attention to the env.IsDevelopment() condition. *The /Error page is meant for non-development viewing only.* As we mentioned back in *Chapter 4* regarding security, always be careful what to show on this page. It may expose system data such as a database connection string that contains credentials or other sensitive data.

To access the exception through the error page, we require the IExceptionHandlerPathFeature instance through HttpContext.Features. This can be seen in the following OnGet() method on the /Error page:

```
public void OnGet()
{
    RequestId = Activity.Current?.Id ?? HttpContext.TraceIdentifier;

    var exceptionFeature =
        HttpContext.Features.Get<IExceptionHandlerPathFeature>();

    // Access the Exception through exceptionFeature?.Error

    // Access the Path through exceptionFeature?.Path
    if (exceptionFeature?.Path == "/")
    {
        ErrorMessage ??= string.Empty;
        ErrorMessage += " We have bigger problems if the main page is
            bombing.";
        _logger.Log(LogLevel.Error, exceptionFeature?.Error,
            ErrorMessage);
    }
}
```

`HttpContext.Features` gives us access to the error. From there, we need to determine what to display on the page. In this case, we can see that the main page contains the error. Once we have identified the issue, we can create a public message, and log the error, and store it in `ErrorMessage` so that the main page can display it.

While this is a simplistic example, alternatively, we can use our middleware to catch global errors as well. Instead of passing in a page location, we can use a Lambda for our exception handling in the middleware, as shown in the following code snippet:

```
app.UseExceptionHandler(handler =>
{
    var logger = loggerFactory.CreateLogger("Middleware");
    handler.Run(async context =>
    {
        context.Response.StatusCode = StatusCodes.
            Status501NotImplemented;
        context.Response.ContentType = MediaTypeNames.Text.Plain;

        await context.Response.WriteAsync("Uh-oh...an exception was
            thrown.");

        var exceptionFeature =
            context.Features.Get<IExceptionHandlerPathFeature>();

        if (exceptionFeature?.Path == "/")
        {
            var message = " Yep, the home page isn't implemented
                yet.";
            await context.Response.WriteAsync(message);
            logger.Log(LogLevel.Error, exceptionFeature.Error,
                $@"Error:{message}");
        }
    });
});
```

We retrieve the `ExceptionHandlerPathFeature` instance the same way as we did on the `/Error` page. Of course, we always want to log the error, so we know what to fix ("It's that darn home page again").

In this section, we learned how to use middleware to create a global exception handler. This allows us to centralize the error handling and avoid too many exception handlers throughout our application. Next, we'll focus on performance considerations when writing exception handlers.

Performance considerations

One common myth about exception handling is that it doesn't affect performance. If exceptions are significantly harming the application's performance, that's a sign that exceptions are being used too much. Exceptions should not control the flow of the application whatsoever.

Ideally, the code should flow with no interruptions. In small web applications with a few users, this type of approach may be adequate, but for high-performing, high-traffic websites, placing a `try/catch` block in frequently-called code may cause the site to suffer a performance hit.

In this section, we covered what exception handling was, reviewed the two types of errors in applications, identified where exception handling is ideal, and covered some of the performance myths regarding exceptions. Next, we'll look at some common exception handling techniques.

Common exception handling techniques

Exceptions are expensive in .NET. When an exception occurs in the application, there are resources in place to begin the error handling process when an exception occurs, such as the stack trace process. Even when we are catching and handling the errors, ASP.NET is still creating the `Exception` object and everything associated with it along with walking up the call stack to locate the handler.

In this section, we'll look at common approaches in the industry to minimize the exceptions through "prevention before exception," why to use logging, why unit testing is similar to exception handling, why empty catch blocks should be avoided, how to simplify exceptions using exception filtering and pattern matching, why blocks are important when releasing resources, and how to rethrow exceptions properly.

Prevention before exception

As we said in the previous section, exceptions interrupt the flow of an application when encountered and can cause more problems than intended, such as releasing resources that were previously allocated and triggering multiple exceptions up the call stack. If we're writing `try/catch` blocks of code to control the flow of the program, we're doing it wrong. It's best to perform checks before wrapping code with `try/catch` blocks.

If there's one thing to take away from this chapter, let it be this principle: prevention before exception.

The concept of prevention before exception refers to the idea of trying to prevent the error from happening using less destructive methods, such as stopping the execution of the website completely.

For example, examine the following code:

```
var number = "2";
int result;
try
{
```

```
        result = int.Parse(number);
    }
catch
    {
        result = 0;
    }
// use result
```

In a happy path, the number will be parsed and the result will be 2. However, if the string contained a value of "hi", the result will become a zero.

A better approach would be using the newest `TryParse` with `var`, as shown here:

```
var number = "2";
if (!int.TryParse(number, out var result))
{
    result = 0;
}
// use result
```

With this approach, we are attempting to convert the number and store the converted value into a new variable called `result`. `TryParse` returns true if the conversion was successful and false if not. If the conversion fails, we set `result` to 0.

We prevented an exception by handling the conversion through easier means. There are a large number of conversion methods in .NET and we can accomplish the same thing without `try`/`catch`/`finally` blocks.

For simpler exceptions, look at the `try`/`catch` block and ask if we can apply some sort of prevention before creating exceptions.

Use logging

When creating a `try`/`catch` block, it's best to show the intent of what we want to get out of the code. Is the error something we can recover from or is it something that requires investigation when it occurs?

If it's the latter, it's best to send a well-constructed error message to the logger before throwing the error. As mentioned in various chapters, it's best to use a logging strategy to identify issues throughout the code base.

If we use the previous example to determine the value that caused the error, we can create a log entry, as shown here:

```
var number = "hi";
int result;
try
{
```

```
    result = int.Parse(number);
}
catch
{
    // gives us "OnGetAsync:invalid number - hi"
    _logger.LogInformation($"{MethodBase.GetCurrentMethod()}:invalid
number - {number}");
    result = 0;
}
// use result
```

While this gives us a clear log entry for our `try/catch` block, we can copy this one-liner to our `TryParse` example as well.

The idea is to provide enough information to developers without jarring the user's experience with errors.

Apply a unit testing methodology

If we have to use a `try/catch` block, look at it like a unit test. We mentioned that unit tests have the triple-A approach (Arrange, Act, and Assert). We want to create a minimal amount of code to get the job done and move on.

Initialize the objects at the beginning (Arrange) and wrap a `try/catch` block around the suspecting line causing the error (Act). Minimize the amount of code inside the `try/catch` block.

Once again, we can apply this approach to the previous code example, which has been modified as follows:

```
// Arrange
var number = "2";
int result;
try
{
    // Act
    result = int.Parse(number);
}
// Assert
catch
{
    // gives us "OnGetAsync:invalid number - hi"
    _logger.LogInformation($"{MethodBase.GetCurrentMethod()}:invalid
number - {number}");
    result = 0;
}
// use result
```

Anything above the `try` statement would be considered part of `Arrange`; the one-liner inside the try's brackets is considered `Act`. The `Assert` piece would be part of the `catch` statement. This statement would be the equivalent of a failed `Assert`.

Avoid empty catch statements

While preventing errors is critical to our applications, consider an empty catch statement, as shown here:

```
private void Deposit(Account myAccount, decimal amount)
{
    try
    {
        myAccount.Deposit(amount);
    }
    catch { }
}
```

What happens when the `Deposit()` method doesn't work? If we do have an error in the code, the `catch` statement should contain something to let the developer know an error occurred. At the very least, a `Log` statement should exist to notify the team about the issue.

While an empty `try`/`catch` block keeps the program from crashing, it causes a bigger problem. Once someone discovers there's an error with depositing funds, it may be hard to find the issue since it doesn't log the problem because it's not logging or throwing an error.

Use exception filtering and pattern matching

If we are dealing with multiple exceptions for a section of code, a new feature in .NET called exception filtering can make the exception handling terser. If we have compact code, exception filtering can provide a more efficient and modern code base.

For instance, file handling can often result in a wide variety of exceptions. Consider the following code snippet:

```
FileStream fileStream = null;
try
{
    fileStream = new FileStream(@"C:\temp\myfile.txt", FileMode.
Append);
}
catch (DirectoryNotFoundException e)
{
    _logger.Log(LogLevel.Information, MethodBase.
GetCurrentMethod()+":Directory not found - " + e.Message);
}
```

```
catch (FileNotFoundException e)
{
    _logger.Log(LogLevel.Information, MethodBase.
GetCurrentMethod()+":File Not Found - " + e.Message);
}
catch (IOException e)
{
    _logger.Log(LogLevel.Information, MethodBase.
GetCurrentMethod()+":I/O Error - " + e.Message);
}
catch (NotSupportedException e)
{
    _logger.Log(LogLevel.Information, MethodBase.
GetCurrentMethod()+":Not Supported - " + e.Message);
}
catch (Exception e)
{
    _logger.Log(LogLevel.Information, MethodBase.
GetCurrentMethod()+":General Exception - " + e.Message);
}
// Use filestream
```

In the preceding code, we log each exception and provide a message based on the specific exception. With exception filtering, we can shorten the lines to something a little easier to read:

```
FileStream fileStream = null;
try
{
    fileStream = new FileStream(@"C:\temp\myfile.txt", FileMode.
Append);
}
catch (Exception e) when
    (  e is DirectoryNotFoundException
    || e is FileNotFoundException)
{
    _logger.Log(LogLevel.Warning, $"{MethodBase.
GetCurrentMethod()}:{nameof(e)} - {e.Message}");
}
catch (Exception e) when
    (e is NotSupportedException
    || e is IOException)
{
    _logger.Log(LogLevel.Error, $"{MethodBase.
GetCurrentMethod()}:{nameof(e)} - {e.Message}");
}
```

```
catch (Exception e)
{
    _logger.Log(LogLevel.Error, $"{MethodBase.
GetCurrentMethod()}:{nameof(e)} - {e.Message}");
}
// Use filestream
```

In the preceding code, we are grouping DirectoryNotFoundException and FileNotFoundException and logging them as warnings. When we encounter a NotSupportedException or IOException error, we consider that a little more of a problem and log those as errors. Anything else coming through will be caught as a general exception and logged as an error with the message.

Along with exception filtering, .NET introduced another new feature called pattern matching. With pattern matching, we can shorten the code even further:

```
FileStream fileStream = null;
try
{
    fileStream = new FileStream(@"C:\temp\myfile.txt", FileMode.
Append);
}
catch (Exception e)
{
    var logLevel = e switch
    {
        DirectoryNotFoundException => LogLevel.Warning,
        FileNotFoundException => LogLevel.Warning,
        _ => LogLevel.Error
    };
    _logger.Log(logLevel, $"{MethodBase.
GetCurrentMethod()}:{nameof(e)} - {e.Message}");
}
// Use filestream
```

The preceding code uses a switch statement inside the catch brackets to identify what type of exception we're experiencing. Think of switch pattern matching as an inline if statement. The preceding line returns the value of logLevel based on the exception type.

The underscore (_) is called a discard variable (it's like a default in a switch statement). If everything else falls through the switch, then we'll just default the log level to LogLevel.Error and log the message with the current method, the name of the exception type, and the exception message.

Exception handling can be wordy with, for instance, I/O-based methods and connections. Exception filtering and pattern matching can help ease the wordiness of catching various exceptions.

Use finally blocks for cleanup

When working with database connections, file-based operations, or resources, it's best to use `finally` for cleanup.

For example, if we're connecting to a database and want to close the connection afterward, we'd have to create a piece of code similar to the following:

```
using System.Data.SqlClient;

var connectionString = @"Data Source=localhost;Initial
Catalog=myDatabase;Integrated Security=true;";
using SqlConnection connection = new SqlConnection(connectionString);

var command = new SqlCommand("UPDATE Users SET Name='Jonathan' WHERE
ID=1 ", connection);
try
{
    command.Connection.Open();
    command.ExecuteNonQuery();
}
catch (SqlException ex)
{
    Console.WriteLine(ex.ToString());
    throw;
}
finally
{
    connection.Close();
}
```

In the preceding code, the connection object is passed into the SqlCommand constructor. When we execute the SQL query, the command is passed into the connection and executed. Once our code is executed, we close the connection in the finally statement. Since we have a using statement and the SqlConnection class implements IDisposable, it will automatically be disposed of.

There are times when we need finally statements to clean up, but there are exceptions when they aren't necessary.

Knowing when to throw

In the previous code example, we issued `throw;` as opposed to `throw ex;`.

If we run the code example in the previous section with `throw;`, we see that the stack trace in Visual Studio is seen through the **Call Stack** pane:

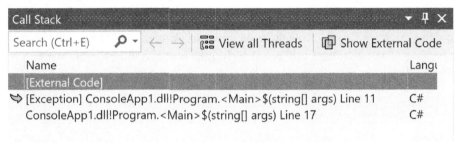

Figure 8.1 – Snapshot of a call stack with a simple throw;

What happens if we change the line to `throw ex;`?

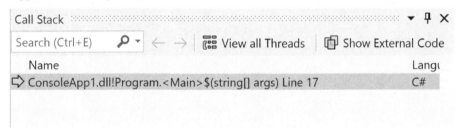

Figure 8.2 – Snapshot of a call stack with throw ex;

The stack trace completely disappears. The error will become harder to track if we don't have a stack trace. There are times when we want to simply throw the exception. It's always better to rethrow the exception so that the stack trace is left intact for locating errors.

In this section, we covered many standards of what is considered practical when applying exception handling in the code. We learned how to minimize exceptions with "prevention before exception," why logging is important, and why exception handling is like unit testing.

We also learned to avoid empty catch blocks, simplify exceptions using exception filtering and pattern matching, when to use finally blocks, and how to rethrow exceptions properly.

Summary

Exception handling is important but requires a level of experience when writing truly robust applications. Applications need to recover so that the user doesn't have a jarring experience.

In this chapter, we learned about exception handling, when to use it, and where it makes sense, as well as performance considerations.

We ended this chapter by learning about the common techniques of exception handling by understanding the "prevention before exception" principle, why logging is important, and why exception handling is like unit testing.

We also learned that empty catch blocks are wasteful, how to simplify exceptions using exception filtering and pattern matching, when to use finally blocks, and how to rethrow exceptions properly.

In the next chapter, we'll look at web API standards and how they are extremely important to the ASP.NET Core ecosystem.

9

Creating Better Web APIs

Web APIs are the essence of the internet. They give developers the openness of the web and the ability to access any data on the internet. However, there are some best practices specific to APIs. The ability to select the right HTTP verb, how to document APIs, and testing APIs are just some of the topics we'll cover.

With that said, the techniques covered in this chapter are vast and dense. We'll try to pack as much information as possible to help build quality APIs. We'll also provide relevant links for further research.

In this chapter, we're going to cover the following main topics:

- Creating APIs quickly
- Designing APIs
- Testing Web APIs
- Standardized Web API techniques

In this chapter, we'll learn how to design, create, test, and document APIs and how to perform full end-to-end tests of our APIs through a CI/CD pipeline.

We'll finish this chapter by reviewing some of the more common techniques for writing APIs, such as using the correct HTTP verbs and status codes, how to avoid large dependent resources, how to implement pagination into APIs, versioning an API, using DTOs instead of entities, and the best way to call other APIs from .NET.

Technical requirements

In .NET 8, Web APIs take a front seat. Visual Studio has added new features to make Web APIs easier to build and test. For this chapter, we recommend using Visual Studio 2022, but the only requirement to view the GitHub repository is a simple text editor.

The code for *Chapter 09* is located in Packt Publishing's GitHub repository, found at `https://github.com/PacktPublishing/ASP.NET-Core-8-Best-Practices`.

Creating APIs quickly

With .NET 8, APIs are integrated into the framework, making it easier to create, test, and document. In this section, we'll learn a quick and easy way to create a minimal API using Visual Studio 2022 and walk through the code it generates. We'll also learn why minimal APIs are the best approach to building REST-based services.

Using Visual Studio

One of the features of .NET 8 is the ability to create minimal REST APIs extremely fast. One way is to use the dotnet command-line tool and the other way is to use Visual Studio. To do so, follow these steps:

1. Open Visual Studio 2022 and create an **ASP.NET Core Web API** project.

2. After selecting the directory for the project, click **Next**.

3. Under the project options, make the following changes:

   - Uncheck the **Use Controllers** option to use minimal APIs

   - Check **Enable OpenAPI support** to include support for API documentation using Swagger:

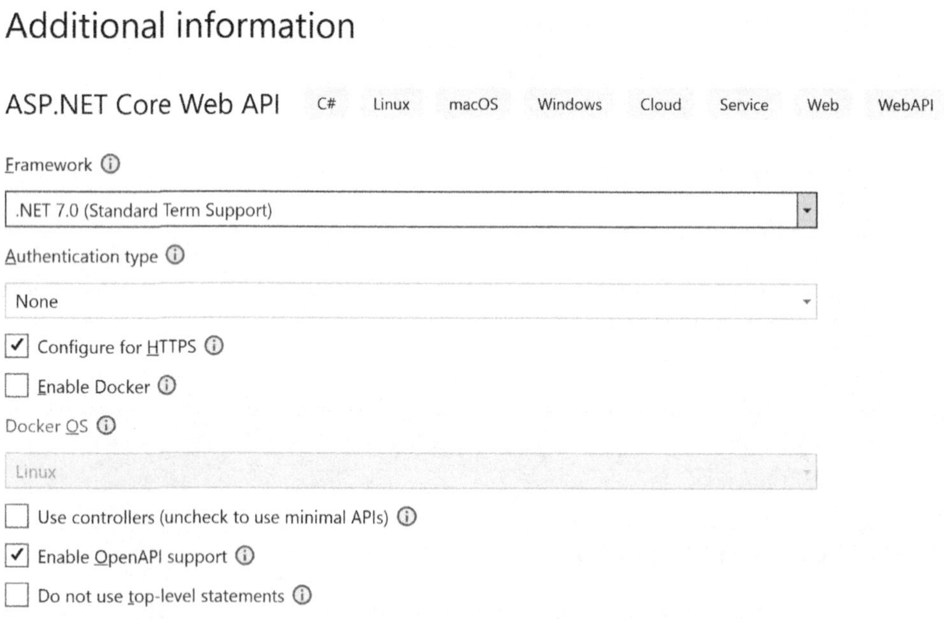

Additional information

ASP.NET Core Web API   C#   Linux   macOS   Windows   Cloud   Service   Web   WebAPI

Framework ⓘ

.NET 7.0 (Standard Term Support)	▾

Authentication type ⓘ

None	▾

☑ Configure for HTTPS ⓘ

☐ Enable Docker ⓘ

Docker OS ⓘ

Linux	▾

☐ Use controllers (uncheck to use minimal APIs) ⓘ

☑ Enable OpenAPI support ⓘ

☐ Do not use top-level statements ⓘ

Figure 9.1 – Options for a web minimal API project

4. Click **Create**.

That's it – we have a simple API! It may not be much of one, but it's still a complete API with Swagger documentation. Swagger is a tool for creating documentation for APIs and implementing the OpenAPI specification, whereas Swashbuckle is a NuGet package that uses Swagger for implementing Microsoft APIs. If we look at the project, there's a single file called `Program.cs`.

5. Opening `Program.cs` will show the entire application. This is one of the strong points of .NET – the ability to create a scaffolded REST API relatively quickly:

```
var builder = WebApplication.CreateBuilder(args);

// Add services to the container.
// Learn more about configuring Swagger/OpenAPI at
    https://aka.ms/aspnetcore/swashbuckle
builder.Services.AddEndpointsApiExplorer();
builder.Services.AddSwaggerGen();

var app = builder.Build();

// Configure the HTTP request pipeline.
if (app.Environment.IsDevelopment())
{
    app.UseSwagger();
    app.UseSwaggerUI();
}

app.UseHttpsRedirection();

var summaries = new[]
{
    "Freezing", "Bracing", "Chilly", "Cool", "Mild",
    "Warm", "Balmy", "Hot", "Sweltering", "Scorching"
};

app.MapGet("/weatherforecast", () =>
{
    var forecast = Enumerable.Range(1, 5).Select(index
    =>
        new WeatherForecast
        (
            DateOnly.FromDateTime(DateTime.Now.AddDays
                (index)),
            Random.Shared.Next(-20, 55),
            summaries[Random.Shared.Next(
```

```
                summaries.Length)]
        ))
        .ToArray();
    return forecast;
})
.WithName("GetWeatherForecast")
.WithOpenApi();

app.Run();

internal record WeatherForecast(DateOnly Date,
int TemperatureC, string? Summary)
{
    public int TemperatureF => 32 +
        (int)(TemperatureC / 0.5556);
}
```

In the preceding code, we created our "application" through the `.CreateBuilder()` method. We also added the `EndpointsAPIExplorer` and `SwaggerGen` services. `EndpointsAPIExplorer` enables the developer to view all endpoints in Visual Studio, which we'll cover later. The `SwaggerGen` service, on the other hand, creates the documentation for the API when accessed through the browser. The next line creates our application instance using the `.Build()` method.

6. Once we have our app instance and we are in development mode, we can add Swagger and the Swagger UI. `.UseHttpsRedirection()` is meant to redirect to HTTPS when the protocol of a web page is HTTP to make the API secure.

7. The next line creates our GET weatherforecast route using `.MapGet()`. We added the `.WithName()` and `.WithOpenApi()` methods to identify the primary method to call and let .NET know it uses the OpenAPI standard, respectively. Finally, we called `app.Run()`.

8. If we run the application, we will see the documented API on how to use our API and what's available. Running the application produces the following output:

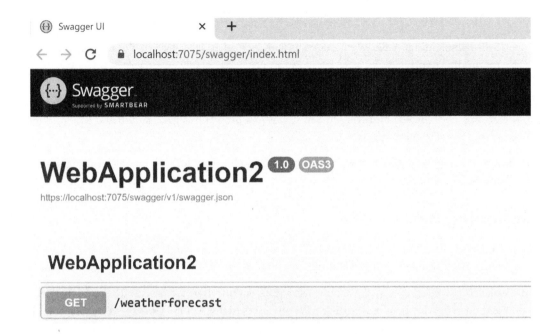

Figure 9.2 – Screenshot of our documented Web API

If we call the /weatherforecast API, we see that we receive JSON back with a 200 HTTP status.

[{"date":"2023-06-12","temperatureC":-8,"summary":"Hot","temperatureF":18},{"date":"2023-06-
13","temperatureC":27,"summary":"Scorching","temperatureF":80},{"date":"2023-06-
14","temperatureC":-16,"summary":"Balmy","temperatureF":4},{"date":"2023-06-
15","temperatureC":48,"summary":"Chilly","temperatureF":118},{"date":"2023-06-
16","temperatureC":-7,"summary":"Bracing","temperatureF":20}]

Figure 9.3 – Results of our /weatherforecast API

Think of this small API as middleware with API controllers combined into one compact file (Program.cs).

Why minimal APIs?

I consider minimal APIs to be a feature in .NET 8, even though it's a language concept. If the application is extremely large, adding minimal APIs should be an appealing feature in four ways:

- **Self-contained**: Simple API functionality inside one file is easy to follow for other developers

- **Performance**: Since we aren't using controllers, the MVC overhead isn't necessary when using these APIs

- **Cross-platform**: With .NET, APIs can now be deployed on any platform
- **Self-documenting**: While we can add Swashbuckle to other APIs, it also builds the documentation for minimal APIs

Moving forward, we'll take these minimal APIs and start looking at Visual Studio's testing capabilities.

In this section, we created and reviewed a minimal API project in Visual Studio and why minimal APIs are important to our projects.

In the next section, we'll look at designing APIs to help eliminate long resource (URL) names and standardized API naming.

Designing APIs

In this section, we'll cover the best approach for delivering intuitive and clear APIs to our users. The design of an API should be well thought-out and make sense when a user wishes to make a request.

To create a truly REST-based API, we must use a different mindset. We have to think of ourselves as a user and not a developer. When writing APIs, the users of the API *are* fellow developers.

Disconnecting from existing schemas

When designing APIs, we need a user's perspective as opposed to basing an API on a class hierarchy or database schema. While developers may consider creating an API based on a class hierarchy or database schema as a shortcut, it could create more complexity as to which resource to use when retrieving data. One example is using an Order resource to find a contact. While an Order entity in Entity Framework Core could contain a `Company` property and we need the contact of the company, we wouldn't write `https://www.myfakesite.com/Order/15/Company/Contact`. Basing a URL structure on an existing hierarchy or schema should be avoided.

It's crucial to disregard existing schemas when designing a sensible API. Look at the API with new eyes to get the best design. The most popular APIs are the cleanest and most intuitive as they use the `collection/item/collection` syntax. A good example of this would be `/orders/15/companys`.

Identifying the resources

In a system, look at how the user interacts with the website and extract the nouns from specific scenarios. These will become the resources for the APIs.

For example, a user can perform the following actions in a shopping cart system:

- View a list of products
- View a product

- Add a product to the cart

- Remove a product from the cart

- Check out

From these scenarios, we can extract the following resources:

- Products

- Product

- Cart

We're starting to identify and logically partition our APIs based on resources used throughout the system.

From here, we can apply an HTTP verb to each resource based on each scenario.

Relating HTTP verbs to resources

Once we have the primary resources, we can apply an HTTP verb to each resource based on the specific scenario we defined in the previous section.

When creating an API, it may be tempting to use the noun/verb syntax – for example, `https://www.myurl.com/products/get` or `https://www.myurl.com/getproducts`. This approach is counterproductive since web standards already exist for this exact purpose.

While this does work, it violates some of the REST principles (which we'll get into when we looked at standardized web API techniques in the following sections). For now, let's take it step by step and create a simple shopping cart API.

Each HTTP verb has a default operation based on its context:

- `GET`: Returns a resource

- `POST`: Creates a new resource

- `PUT`: Replaces an entire resource based on an identifier

- `PATCH`: Updates specific items in a resource based on an identifier

- `DELETE`: Deletes a resource

For example, our scenarios in the previous section can begin to take shape based on the resources and their verbs:

- `GET /api/products`: View a list of products

- `GET /api/product/{id}`: View a product

- `POST /api/cart/{cartId}`: Add a product to the cart with `POST` data (that is, `new { ProductId = {productId}, Qty = 1 })`

- `PATCH /api/cart/{cartId}`: Remove a product from the cart with `POST` data (that is, `new { ProductId = {productId} })`

- `GET /api/cart/{cartId}`: Retrieve a cart with all the products in the cart

- `POST /api/cart/{cartId}/checkout`: Check out

Once we have matched the resources to the scenarios that have been defined, we can move forward with returning status codes to the caller.

Returning HTTP status codes

With the resources defined, we need to know whether the request was successful or not. This is where we return HTTP status codes.

These status codes are broken into the following categories:

- **1xx**: Information codes

- **2xx**: Success codes

- **3xx**: Redirection codes

- **4xx**: Client-side codes

- **5xx**: Server errors

Similar to unit tests, we look at a "happy" path and a broken path. But with APIs, we need to add an unrecoverable path in case an unrecoverable error occurs.

Let's look at two of the URLs and what status codes they should return.

`GET /api/products` will return the following status codes:

- **200 Success**: Products were successfully returned

- **500 Internal Server Error**: Optional if something caused a problem

If the API was successful, it will return a list of the products with a 200 status code. If there are issues, it will return a 500 status code. The API could also return additional status codes. For example, if an API call is made for specific users, the API could return a 401, which is an Unauthorized status code.

`POST /api/cart/{cartId}` with a post body of (`new { ProductId = {productId}, Qty = 1 }`) will return the following status codes:

- **201 Created**: The item was created and added to the cart
- **202 Accepted**: The item was added to the cart
- **404 Not Found**: The cart or product wasn't found
- **500 Internal Server Error**: An unrecoverable error occurred

With this API, we can return either a 201 Created or a 202 Accepted status code. If we couldn't find the cart or product to add to the cart, return a 404 status code. Otherwise, return a 500 status code.

While these two examples are not set in stone, they should provide a template for the team to discuss what business rules dictate the status codes that are returned to the user. Whatever status codes are returned, they should provide enough context as to the request made through the API.

Some APIs seen in the wild use an all-or-nothing approach; they either return a 200 or a 500. It depends on how much information we want to send back to the client. These types of APIs feel like they're missing more functionality, such as Unauthorized (401) or Not Found (404) status codes. It's a best practice to include as much information as we can to the caller of the API.

> **HTTP status codes**
>
> HTTP status codes are standard in web development and are presented through the RFC **Request for Comments (RFC)** 9110 proposal located at `https://www.rfc-editor.org/rfc/rfc9110#status.codes`. Luckily, we don't need to memorize them all since .NET provides a `HttpStatusCodeEnum` class with every status code at `https://learn.microsoft.com/en-us/dotnet/api/system.net.httpstatuscode`, along with `IActionResults` such as `Ok(object)`. Specific status codes can be found at `https://learn.microsoft.com/en-us/dotnet/api/microsoft.aspnetcore.http.results.statuscode`.

In this section, we learned how to design APIs and broke down each step – that is, disconnecting from the technology, identifying the resources, knowing the right verbs to apply to resources, and providing the correct response codes to our API.

In the next section, we will look at two ways to test our APIs: one in Visual Studio with the new Endpoints Explorer and the other by creating a complete integration test.

Testing Web APIs

Once we have our APIs designed and created, we need a way to test them in our IDE and our integration tests. Luckily, Visual Studio has added the new Endpoints Explorer.

In this section, we'll learn two ways to test our APIs. One way is through our development environment using Visual Studio. The second way we'll test our API is through integration tests. If we have a CI/CD pipeline (which we should from *Chapter 2*), these will automatically run to confirm our APIs work as expected.

Visual Studio Endpoints Explorer

Historically, developers using Visual Studio had to run a separate tool to test their APIs, but with the latest version of .NET 8, the Visual Studio team added a new panel called **Endpoints Explorer**:

Figure 9.4 – Endpoints Explorer

If we have a collection of APIs defined in the `Program.cs` file, our collection will appear as follows:

Figure 9.5 – Collection of APIs in Endpoints Explorer

Right-clicking on an API will generate a request in a new HTTP Editor. The HTTP Editor allows custom-defined variables for the APIs listed:

```
GET {{hostAddress}}/attractions
        @hostAddress = https://localhost:7218

        // Get all attractions
    GET {{hostAddress}}/attractions
        Content-Type: application/json

    ###

        // Get all locations
        GET {{hostAddress}}/locations

        ###
```

Figure 9.6 – Sample API collection in the HTTP Editor

In *Figure 9.6*, the HTTP Editor uses the following commands to issue HTTP requests:

- @: Creates a variable for the file (for example, `@variable = value`)
- //: This specifies comments
- ###: This specifies the end of an HTTP request
- <HTTP Verb>: Creates a REST-based request, including DELETE, GET, HEAD, OPTIONS, PATCH, POST, PUT, and TRACE requests
- <Headers>: Adds headers directly after defining the URL so that they're included in the request

Once we have defined the APIs, there are green arrows in the left gutter. Run the application to test the API locally. Pressing the arrow in the far left gutter *while the API is running* will produce results in the right-hand pane:

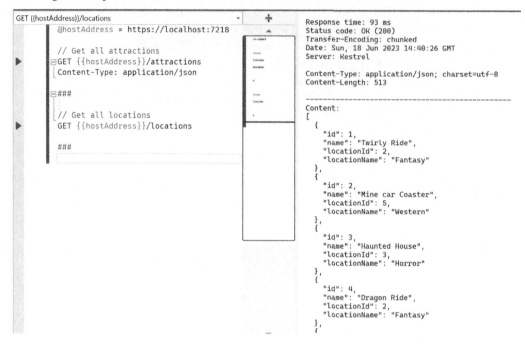

Figure 9.7 – Results of the /attractions request

In this example, we tested the /attractions request, received the data, and displayed it on the right.

Why is this important?

By using this new Visual Studio feature, we gain the following advantages:

- **Centralized APIs**: We have a catalog of all of our APIs in one place
- **Self-documented**: Developers new to the project can find this .http file, execute sample requests, and understand what each API does in the system
- **IDE-integrated**: Additional tools aren't necessary for testing our APIs

This new feature is extremely helpful to developers looking to test existing APIs locally and also complements new minimal APIs introduced into the system.

> **Additional Endpoints Explorer material**
>
> For additional material on Endpoints Explorer, Sayed Ibrahim Hashimi has provided a great write-up about everything it can do at `https://devblogs.microsoft.com/visualstudio/web-api-development-in-visual-studio-2022/#endpoints-explorer`.

In this section, we learned about Endpoints Explorer, how we can use it to help test APIs locally, and why it's important. In the next section, we'll take our APIs and learn how to use integration tests to produce quick results.

Integration testing APIs

In the previous section, we learned about how to use Endpoints Explorer to test our APIs. However, we shouldn't have to install Visual Studio on a server to test our APIs.

In this section, we will look at applying an integration server for our APIs to achieve a complete end-to-end test.

When we created unit tests back in *Chapter 8*, we created an in-memory representation of a database. We can create a similar environment where we can spin up and tear down the entire environment for API tests.

In our CI/CD pipelines, we can build a disposable server for our integration tests to provide a full end-to-end test with APIs and services and a disposable database.

Building the integration server

Since .NET provides us with a simple `Program.cs` file for our applications, we can wrap the entire application and replace the services we want to mimic with a web and database server.

We can set up the environment using the `WebApplicationFactory` class. We include the minimal API project as a dependency in our `Api.Tests` project. Once we have our dependency in the program, we can create our `WebApplicationFactory` class:

```
using System.Data.Common;
using Microsoft.AspNetCore.Mvc.Testing;
using Microsoft.EntityFrameworkCore;
using Microsoft.EntityFrameworkCore.Storage;
using Microsoft.Extensions.DependencyInjection;
using Microsoft.Extensions.DependencyInjection.Extensions;
using Microsoft.Extensions.Hosting;
using ThemePark.Data.DataContext;
```

```
namespace ThemePark.Api.Tests;

public class TestThemeParkApiApplication :
WebApplicationFactory<Program>
{
    protected override IHost CreateHost(
    IHostBuilder builder)
    {
        var root = new InMemoryDatabaseRoot();

        builder.ConfigureServices(services =>
        {
            services.RemoveAll(typeof(
                DbContextOptionsBuilder<ThemeParkDbContext>
                ));

            services.AddScoped(sp => new
            DbContextOptionsBuilder<ThemeParkDbContext>()
                .UseInMemoryDatabase("TestApi", root)
                .UseApplicationServiceProvider(sp)
                .Options);

            services.AddDbContext<ThemeParkDbContext>(
            (container, options) =>
            {
                var connection = container
                    .GetRequiredService<DbConnection>();
                options.UseSqlite(connection);
            });

            services.AddTransient<IThemeParkDbContext,
                ThemeParkDbContext>();
        });

        return base.CreateHost(builder);
    }
}
```

In the preceding code example, we inherited from `WebApplicationFactory<Program>`. The generic `<Program>` comes from the included dependency we referenced. Then, we created a root for our in-memory database and proceeded to configure our services by removing all instances of `DbContextOptionsBuilder<ThemeParkDbContext>`. Once we've removed these, we can create a new scoped reference to the same type with our updated settings for the database.

Next, we added our new `ThemeParkDbContext` with our updated connection using a SQLite database. Remember, Entity Framework Core will automatically create the structure of our entire database with the `.EnsureCreated()` method. Finally, we added a dependency injection registration for `IThemeParkDbContext` for the services in our application.

That's it for our integration server. Now, we can use `TestThemeParkApiApplication` in our integration test. For example, if we want to create a test for our `/attractions` API, our integration test will look as follows:

```
using Microsoft.Extensions.DependencyInjection;
using ThemePark.Data.DataContext;

namespace ThemePark.Api.Tests;

[TestClass]
public class ApiTests
{
    private TestThemeParkApiApplication _app;

    [TestInitialize]
    public void Setup()
    {
        _app = new TestThemeParkApiApplication();
        using (var scoped = _app.Services.CreateScope())
        {
            var context = scoped.ServiceProvider
                .GetService<IThemeParkDbContext>();
            context?.Database.EnsureCreated();
        }
    }


    [TestMethod]
    [TestCategory("Integration")]
    public async Task GetAllAttractions()
    {
        // Arrange
        var client = _app.CreateClient();
        var expected = TestData.ExpectedAttractionData;
```

```
        // Act
        var response = await
            client.GetAsync("/attractions");
        var actual = await response.Content
            .ReadAsStringAsync();

        // Assert
        Assert.AreEqual(expected, actual);
    }
}
```

In the preceding code snippet, we initialized `TestThemeParkApiApplication` on setup so that every instance is new through the `.EnsureCreated()` method. `_app.CreateClient` gives us `HttpClient` to make a call to a URL. We make a call to our `/attractions` API and compare it with a resource string we created instead of cluttering our test methods with large JSON strings. Finally, our test compares the JSON results with what's returned from an API.

The ability to create entire front-to-back integration tests proving the APIs, Entity Framework queries, and database code work as expected while running through a CI/CD pipeline with successful tests should instill confidence about the code.

In this section, we learned how to take APIs and test them in Visual Studio's Endpoints Explorer. We also learned how to take those APIs and make them testable in a CI/CD pipeline by wrapping our API project using `WebApplicationFactory`.

In the next section, we'll cover some of the common practices used in the industry when building APIs.

Standardized Web API techniques

In this section, we'll learn how to use HTTP verbs and status codes properly, how to avoid large dependent resources, how to create paginations for APIs, how to version an API, using DTOs instead of entities, and the best way to make API calls from .NET.

Using the right HTTP verbs and status codes

So far, we've looked at how to use HTTP verbs and how to return status codes. While this may seem like a trivial thing, some systems ignore these standards and use POSTs all the time, regardless of the function.

Swagger provides a great template for documenting APIs and with Visual Studio's new Endpoints Explorer, Visual Studio brings this fundamental documentation down to the developer's IDE, making the API easier to read and implement in other projects, showing developers what verbs to use and what status codes are expected.

In our example of a shopping cart API earlier in this chapter, users were going to add products to a cart and proceed to check out. They were going to use a cart to begin this process. The function of checking out led us to use the cart API with a method of checkout (`/cart/checkout`), which makes perfect sense. We should take the user's actions and match them to actions in the APIs.

Beware dependent resources

But how far do I take my API based on resources? What if one resource belongs to another resource and that's dependent on another resource, and so on?

Here's an example: `/users/{userId}/projects/{projectId}/tasks`.

We want to get a user's tasks for a project, but this URL seems a bit long, doesn't it? How do we break this down into something a bit more manageable? Anything more than three levels deep is simply asking for trouble.

This URL requires a more granular approach – that is, breaking out each resource. Instead of the preceding URL, a better approach would be to use `/users/{userId}/projects` to retrieve a list of projects a user is working on at a time. The next URL would provide the tasks based on the selected project and look like `/projects/{projectId}/tasks`.

As developers, we all know everything is a compromise. In this case, we are providing a simpler API but requiring two calls instead of one.

These are discussions to be had with team members, but essentially, the smaller the URL, the easier it is to implement. The longer the URL, the more resource lookups are necessary to fulfill the request.

Pagination in API results

For most API calls, results are returned in a raw, **JavaScript Object Notation** (**JSON**) format, usually as a collection or a single item. What if the client side needs paginated results and they only want one page of data for now?

To assist client-side developers, a JSON result could contain the following:

```
{
    "total": 7,
    "pageSize": 7,
    "currentPage": 1,
    "next": false,
    "previous": false,
    "results": [
        {
            "id": 1,
            "name": "Twirly Ride",
```

```
            "locationId": 2,
            "locationName": "Fantasy"
        },
        {

            "id": 2,
            "name": "Mine car Coaster",
            "locationId": 5,
        .
        .
```

While returning results as a collection is usually required, some fields to return in the header are as follows:

- `Total`: Total number of records

- `PageSize`: How many records are returned in this response

- `TotalPages`: Specifies the total number of pages based on `PageSize`

- `CurrentPage`: Specifies what page we are currently on

- `Next` and `Previous`: Are there enough records to move back and forward?

- `Sort`: Specifies how the results are sorted

- `Filter`: Specifies what filter was applied to the results

The header is meant to help our fellow client-side developer make the most of the response. While this isn't a comprehensive list of fields to include, it should be implemented with consistency across every single response when displaying a subset of records on the client.

A "status code" field or "success" field in the header should be avoided since HTTP status codes are considered the expected response.

Versioning APIs

When creating APIs, by default, they'll more than likely be in a raw state with no versioning in place. There are four types of versioning:

- **No versioning**: When we create our first API

- **URI versioning**: Placing another segment into the URL is extremely common and recommended (/v1/users)

- **Query string**: This involves appending a query string to the end of the URL (/users/?version=1)

- **Header versioning**: This involves using `custom-header` to place the version into the header:

```
GET /users
Custom-Header: api-version=1
```

The most common versioning technique that's used is URI versioning. While everyone's mileage may vary, this technique is appealing because it's immediately obvious which version we're using.

Use DTOs, not entities!

While testing our API, we weren't returning entities (`Attraction` or `Location`). Instead, we were returning **data transfer objects** (**DTOs**), which are a subset of properties.

Our security chapter (*Chapter 4*) mentioned not to expose too much when it comes to primary keys or sensitive information. DTOs give the developer a chance to pick and choose which properties should be exposed to the client.

For example, our `Attraction` DTO is meant to provide a minimal amount of information; we'll discuss this after we look at the following code example:

```
public static class AttractionExtensions
{
    public static AttractionDto ToDto(
    this Attraction attraction)
    {
        return new AttractionDto
        {
            Id = attraction.Id,
            Name = attraction.Name,
            LocationId = attraction.LocationId,
            LocationName = attraction.Location == null
                ? string.Empty
                : attraction.Location.Name
        };
    }
}
```

Here, we have a simplified `AttractionDto` class containing simple properties. We also have a `LocationName` property based on our dependent `Location` class.

While we have this as a `.ToDto()` method, we could create other DTO extension methods to return different data in a `.ToDifferentDto()` method or whatever we want to call it.

Another reason to use DTOs instead of Entity Framework entities is the potentially recursive nature of navigational properties. When an entity is returned from an API, it's turned into a JSON object. If we have a nested entity, it'll follow it down the chain. It's better to isolate and distill an entity's properties down to their native types for basic consumption on the client side when they're returned from the API.

Avoid new instances of HttpClient

While the majority of this chapter discussed creating and testing APIs, I feel we need to mention how to consume them in a .NET application as well.

There are various ways to consume a web API, such as using `WebRequest` or `WebClient`, but for most purposes, the use of the `HttpClient` class is recommended because of its flexibility and modernization. The `WebRequest` and `WebClient` classes were included for the transition of legacy applications. With that said, it's easy to create a new instance of `HttpClient`, but it's not the best approach.

Microsoft states that `HttpClient` should only be used once per the lifetime of an application. If we create instances of `HttpClient` in multiple locations in our application, we are hindering the performance and scalability opportunities. It causes an issue called TCP port exhaustion if the rate of requests is too high, so it's best to avoid code such as the following:

```
// Bad use of HttpClient
var client = new HttpClient();
```

Some developers may take this a step further and decide the following code snippet is better by wrapping a `using` statement to dispose of an `HttpClient` class properly:

```
// Still not good
using (var client = new HttpClient())
{
    .

    .
}
```

The problem with this code is that we're still creating another instance of `HttpClient`, still causing port exhaustion, and still disposing of it when we'll more than likely need it later.

In .NET Core 2.1, Microsoft created an `IHttpClientFactory` class to deliver a single instance of `HttpClient`. We can simply ask it for an `HttpClient` instance and we'll receive one. The best news is it can be dependency injected.

The code becomes easier to work with once we've injected the class through constructors, as shown in the following code snippet:

```
public class IndexModel : PageModel
{
    private readonly ILogger<IndexModel> _logger;
    private readonly IHttpClientFactory _factory;

    public IndexModel(
        ILogger<IndexModel> logger,
        IHttpClientFactory factory)
    {
        _logger = logger;
        _factory = factory;
    }

    public async Task OnGet()
    {
        // Bad use of HttpClient
        // var client = new HttpClient();

        // Still not good
        //using (var client = new HttpClient())
        //{
        //      .
        //      .
        //}

        // Best way to use HttpClient
        var client = _factory.CreateClient();

        // use client.GetAsync("https://www.google.com") to
            grab HTML
    }
}
```

When we ask `HttpClientFactory` for a client using `.CreateClient()`, it won't create a new instance of `HttpClient` unless it has to.

Think of the `.CreateClient()` method as using a singleton design pattern behind the scenes, similar to the code shown here:

```
private static HttpClient _client { get; set; }

public HttpClient CreateClient()
{
    if (_client == null)
    {
        _client = new HttpClient();
    }

    return _client;
}
```

As a side note, the preceding code is *not* thread-safe; it has been provided to show the concept of a singleton design pattern.

We always get an instance of `HttpClient`, which is a better way to make server-side API calls.

Summary

In this chapter, we learned about several techniques, such as how to design an API by disconnecting from technology by becoming a user of the application, identifying the resources, and using the right HTTP verbs and correct status codes. We also learned how to create, test, and document APIs, along with why minimal APIs are important. After, we learned how to use the new Endpoints Explorer in Visual Studio 2022, as well as how to build an automated end-to-end test of our APIs in a CI/CD pipeline.

Once we understood the process of writing APIs, we examined what standards were used in the industry to create common and useful APIs, such as using the correct HTTP verbs and status codes, avoiding large URLs, how to use pagination with APIs, versioning our API, using DTOs instead of entities, and the optimal way to use `HttpClient` when making API calls from .NET.

In the next chapter, we'll look at how to improve performance across various topics we've covered in this book, and we'll also provide some new performance tips.

10
Push Your Application with Performance

With each new release of **ASP.NET**, the ASP.NET team continues to make performance a priority. When ASP.NET Core introduced a different way of building web applications with streamlined enhancements (including **middleware** and **Razor Pages**) the focus was continually on improving the C# language as well. These technologies are what give ASP.NET its spark and speed.

ASP.NET is cross-platform, has built-in support for dependency injection, is open source, and is one of the fastest-performing frameworks in the industry.

While this is an ASP.NET book with a chapter on performance, there will be additional aspects of web development that are equally as important. We'll stay focused on ASP.NET and C# performance as much as possible.

In this chapter, we're going to cover the following main topics:

- Why Performance Matters
- Establishing Baselines
- Applying Performance Best Practices

By the end of this chapter, you'll understand the importance of performance in your application, how to establish client-side and server-side baselines and techniques on how to optimize the client-side resources for faster delivery, and finally, how to deliver content faster with server-side performance techniques such as optimizing HTML, implementing various caching techniques, and identifying slow queries.

Technical requirements

When creating baselines and testing performance for your web application, there is a need for an IDE or editor you feel comfortable with for writing code. We recommend using your favorite editor to view the GitHub repository. Our recommendations include the following:

- **Visual Studio** (preferably the latest version)
- **Visual Studio Code**
- **JetBrains Rider**

The code for this chapter is located in Packt Publishing's GitHub repository, located at `https://github.com/PacktPublishing/ASP.NET-Core-8-Best-Practices`.

Why Performance Matters

Performance takes many shapes and forms in web development since there are so many moving pieces to make a website always ready and available to our users. As a developer, if someone asked for help regarding a website being slow, what advice would you recommend? It's a tough question to answer verbally without examining the website. With websites, there may be times when performance isn't just one technology; the problem may be more than one bottleneck.

For instance, when loading a web page in the browser, do you see content appear, but images take a long time and paint row by row? How about accessing the database? Do you have slow queries where the server takes a minute to retrieve records? Are web APIs performing at more than two seconds for each request?

As you can see, performance is an analysis of an entire website including browser, server, C#, API, and database.

Amazon published a study calculating that if a page load slowed down by even 1 second on their website, it could cost them $1.6B in sales.

> **How one second could cost Amazon $1.6 billion in sales**
>
> The research was reported by Fast Company and is located at `https://fastcompany.com/1825005/how-one-second-could-cost-amazon-16-billion-sales`.

While this is a head-turner, there is a more recent article on how Netflix replaced React with plain JavaScript (more commonly called Vanilla JavaScript). This provided huge gains in performance. In the case study, it reported one page had 300 KB of JavaScript, which is a lot. However, compared to other websites such as `CNN.com` (4.4 MB of JavaScript) and `USAToday.com` (1.5 MB of JavaScript), 300 KB of JavaScript is considered minimal.

> **A Netflix web performance case study**
>
> Google Chrome Engineering Lead *Addy Osmani* wrote an article about the performance gains Netflix experienced through optimizations. The case study can be found at `https://medium.com/dev-channel/a-netflix-web-performance-case-study-c0bcde26a9d9`.

With these specific scenarios and case studies, many companies took notice and focused primarily on performance. Even Microsoft focused its efforts on performance by submitting its results to TechEmpower's industry framework benchmark results. As a result of the constant improvement, ASP.NET is now ranked as one of the fastest platforms for the web.

> **TechEmpower framework benchmark results**
>
> Every year, TechEmpower updates its results in a chart that can be found at `https://techempower.com/benchmarks/`. As of July 19, 2022, ASP.NET is ranked #9 in performance.

Finally, with Google as the most dominant player in the search engine industry, it attached how fast a page loads to your **search engine result pages** (**SERPs**). Translation: the speed of your site is one of the ranking factors for how high you are in the search results (which we'll discuss in the next section).

> **Google using site speed in web search ranking**
>
> On Google's blog, they mentioned that page speed is another factor taken into account when ranking your website. The post is found at `https://developers.google.com/search/blog/2010/04/using-site-speed-in-web-search-ranking`.

Performance is one of my favorite topics. The idea of making small changes that lead to large performance gains is definitely exciting. It also can be visually apparent as well. This chapter is meant to assist in using techniques and tools to identify those performance issues on any website.

The good news is, in past chapters, we've already mentioned specific ways to improve performance that we'll refer back to when relevant. As I've said in *Chapter 4*, performance should be the top priority when building ASP.NET web applications, with security running a close second.

Performance has always been a mix between an art and a science as you'll see in some of the sections in this chapter. There is *perceived* performance and then there's *actual* performance.

Actual performance is a measurement when an activity or task immediately responds and notifies the user that it's finished. An immediate response is a goal. Perceived performance is a subjective measurement where users experience an activity or task as quick, even when it isn't. One example of perceived performance is when the user requests a web page and the browser renders the page immediately. The content continues to load in the background while keeping the user's focus by allowing them to scroll through the page waiting for the additional content. As a result, users think the site is "fast" because it responded immediately. Spinners and progress bars are other ways to achieve perceived performance while something is processing.

While perceived performance is a way to divert a user's attention while waiting for a process to complete, this chapter will focus more on actual performance.

In the next section, we'll learn how to create baselines for client-side and server-side code using public web tools and specific server tools such as **Visual Studio Performance Profiler**, **Benchmark.net**, and **Application Insights**.

Establishing Baselines

So, how do you know you're experiencing a slowdown on a website? Is it because of a recent release of a software product, or a new NuGet package installed causing the slowdown?

While identifying an issue, you may be asking yourself, "what changed?" But the question everyone *should* be asking is "how do you measure performance?" In order to measure it, there needs to be a baseline of what's expected when it comes to performance.

Each part of your application should include performance tests. Whether it's the frontend, a C# subsystem, a web API, or the database, the proper systems should be in place to notify the team when a system isn't performing as expected.

Using Client-Side Tools

Issues on the client side are mostly due to load times, delivery of resources not found (such as HTML pages, images, CSS, and JavaScript), or JavaScript errors in general. However, this doesn't mean the entire problem is on the client.

Creating a baseline for your client-side code should be conducted through a testing tool such as **Cypress** or **Selenium** during development and recording the duration of tests. Compare the latest scenarios with previous test results to see where there is a time difference.

Another approach for determining a baseline is to use various tools on the web such as the tools listed in this section. Think of these tools as like taking your car to the mechanic for maintenance. These tools scan your public website, analyze all aspects of the site, and provide a report on how to fix each issue found.

Some of the tools to give you insights into the performance of a website include the following:

- **Google PageSpeed Insights** (`https://pagespeed.web.dev`): Google uses its search engine to rank your site and provides an exceptional tool to help with website problems.

- **Lighthouse** (`https://developer.chrome.com/docs/lighthouse/`): If your site isn't publicly accessible to analyze from one of these tools, you can use the Lighthouse extension to run tests on the site in-house. Lighthouse produces a full report of recommendations on how to make your site perform better.

- **GTMetrix** (`https://gtmetrix.com`): GTMetrix is a tool I've been using over the years and it continues to impress and improve each year. It provides a performance summary, speed visualization, and recommendations.

- **Google Search Console** (`https://search.google.com/search-console`): Google created this for administrators of websites to identify performance issues along with other general maintenance tools, such as what people are typing into Google to find your website.

- **DevTools**: DevTools is a panel of web developer tools located inside of Google Chrome, Mozilla Firefox, Apple Safari, and Microsoft Edge to help web developers analyze web pages, and it's becoming the IDE of the internet. Pressing F12 in the browser will open the panel.

These tools are great for gauging how well your site performs on the internet and how it performs based on the last revision. If your last release takes 0.5 seconds to load and the latest release now takes three seconds, it's time to examine what changed. What better way to check this than to automate the process (refer to *Chapter 2*) by reporting on the performance issue before deploying the site?

Using Server-Side Tools

With ASP.NET, creating baselines for your code is just as easy with a number of tools at your disposal.

In this section, we'll review some of the tools available for creating a baseline for your code such as Visual Studio, Benchmark.net, Application Insights, and other tools such as NDepend.

Visual Studio Performance Tools

With Visual Studio being a solid IDE in the industry, the ability to gauge C# performance was becoming more prevalent because if code was slow, developers wanted a way to locate the bottleneck.

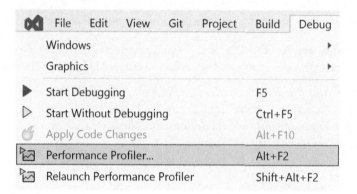

Figure 10.1 – Performance Profiler in Visual Studio 2022

When starting **Performance Profiler**, you're presented with a list of options:

Available Tools

□ .NET Async ⑦
Tool to investigate async/await usage in .NET applications

□ .NET Object Allocation Tracking ⚙ ⑦
See where .NET Objects are allocated and when they are reclaimed by the GC

□ Database ⑦
Examine when queries were executed and measure how long they take

□ File IO ⑦
See what File I/O operations are being performed, how long they take, and how much data they're processing

□ Memory Usage ⚙ ⑦
Investigate application memory to find issues such as memory leaks

□ .NET Counters ⚙ ⑦
Tool to visualize performance counters in .NET applications

□ CPU Usage ⚙ ⑦
See where the CPU is spending time executing your code. Useful when the CPU is the performance bottleneck

□ Events Viewer ⚙ ⑦
See the events (ETW or NetTrace) that occurred during the session, such as log messages, exceptions and HTTP requests

□ Instrumentation ⚙ ⑦
See precise timing and call counts of functions in your code

Figure 10.2 – List of available options before running Performance Profiler

As you can see, there are a vast number of options crossing multiple touchpoints. For example, there is a **Database** option to look at how your queries are performing in the application.

The metrics for databases are similar to the **Entity Framework** details explaining the duration it took to execute the query. Another option is identifying where async/await problems can occur as well as memory usage and object allocation.

Benchmark.net

If there are smaller, self-contained methods required to test, one of the best tools around for micro-benchmarking is Benchmark.net (`https://benchmarkdotnet.org/`).

Benchmark.net takes specific methods and tests them with different scenarios. The one caveat to this is that the Benchmark project *must* be a console application.

As an example, if we wanted to test the age-old debate as to which is faster between string concatenation or a `StringBuilder` class, we would write two benchmark tests to determine which was faster, as shown in the following:

```
public class Benchmarks
{
    [Benchmark(Baseline = true)]
    public void StringConcatenationScenario()
    {
        var input = string.Empty;
        for (int i = 0; i < 10000; i++)
        {
            input += «a»;
        }
    }

    [Benchmark]
    public void StringBuilderScenario()
    {
        var input = new StringBuilder();
        for (int i = 0; i < 10000; i++)
        {
            input.Append(«a»);
        }
    }
}
```

In the preceding code, we created a string in one scenario and an instance of a `StringBuilder()` class in another. To accomplish the same goal, we add 10,000 'a's and start the benchmark.

Based on the results in *Figure 10.3*, the obvious choice is to use `StringBuilder()` for performing large string concatenations:

Method	Mean	Error	StdDev	Ratio
StringConcatenationScenario	51,694.5 us	3,464.50 us	10,215.14 us	1.000
StringBuilderScenario	122.9 us	4.97 us	14.35 us	0.002

Figure 10.3 – Comparing the performance of a string concatenation versus a StringBuilder() class

In regards to creating a baseline, we added an additional parameter to our `[Benchmark]` attribute in our first scenario, called `Baseline`, and set it to `true`. This tells Benchmark.net to use this as our baseline when measuring the performance of our other methods. You can have any number of methods to achieve the same result, but everything will be compared to the one method with `Baseline=true` in the Benchmark attribute.

For small, compact methods, Benchmark.net is definitely a great tool for providing insight into ways to create faster code using micro-optimizations.

Application Insights

Microsoft's Application Insights is meant to be a general-purpose analysis tool for collecting telemetry about everything your application does. Once set up, Application Insights can collect data about the following:

- Requests – web pages and API calls

- Dependencies – what is your application loading behind the scenes?

- Exceptions – every exception your application throws

- Performance counters – automatically identifying slowdowns

- Heartbeats – is the application still up and running?

- Logs – a centralized location for collecting all types of logs for your application

When adding Application Insights, Application Insights *does* require an Azure subscription.

Application Insights additional material

There are various ways to set up Application Insights and way too many to cover in this chapter. For more information on Application Insights and how to set it up for your application, navigate to `https://learn.microsoft.com/en-us/azure/azure-monitor/app/asp-net-core`.

Some other recommendations for creating baselines and identifying bottlenecks include the following:

- **JetBrains dotTrace/dotMemory** – dotTrace is a performance profiler tool, and dotMemory is a memory profiler tool. Both are exceptional tools and perform deep dives into how well your application performs. dotTrace and dotMemory give you the ability to compare a baseline of results against another set of results ("comparing snapshots").

- **RedGate ANTS Performance Profiler/Memory Profiler** – With the ability to profile .NET code and memory allocations, the ANTS Performance and Memory Profiler demonstrates a similar approach to performance and memory profiling while conducting a deep-dive analysis while your code is running.

- **NDepend** – The first time you run NDepend against your code, you immediately create a baseline of your code. The next time you run NDepend, it compares your baseline to the new code you wrote and, as an example, can provide data on "too many exceptions raised" or cyclomatic complexity (which is how complex your code is based on conditional branching, such as `if..else` or switches). These can be user-defined as well to meet your code quality requirements using **Code Query for LINQ** (**CQLinq**). NDepend also has capabilities to integrate into your CI/CD pipeline to automate the process.

- **Build-it-yourself metrics** – Back in *Chapter 7*, we explained how to "identify slow integration tests." Using the diagnostic Stopwatch on your unit, integration, and APIs, you can perform and report on these metrics even before sending out a release.

When these tools examine your application, they perform analysis on how to optimize your code by finding hotspots. If the hotspot is called enough times, your application's performance will suffer. The path to get to this hotspot is called the **hot path**.

Databases

While you can create a baseline with databases, most optimizations are done at the database level by analyzing stored procedures, index management, and schema definitions. Each database type has its own performance tools for finding bottlenecks. For now, we'll focus specifically on **SQL Server** tools.

SQL Server Management Studio (SSMS) Profiler

With **SSMS** using a profiler interface, developers have the ability to identify whether a particular ad-hoc query, stored procedure, or table isn't performing as expected.

SQL Server Profiler is located under the **Tools** option as the first menu item, as shown in *Figure 10.4*:

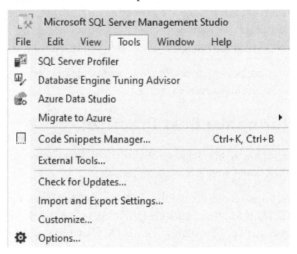

Figure 10.4 – SQL Server Profiler in SSMS

On running SQL Server profiler, every request sent to the database is logged along with how long it took, how many reads and writes are necessary, and the results returned.

Query Store

One of the latest features of SQL Server 2016 is the **Query Store**. The Query Store provides you with insight into how to improve performance on SQL Server.

Once enabled (right-click on database | **Properties** | **Query Store** | **Operation Mode: On**), it'll begin analyzing your SQL Server workload when actively being used and make recommendations on how to improve performance.

Once the data is collected, the metrics are available using stored procedures to identify slow-performing queries.

> **Query Store additional material**
>
> For additional material on Microsoft's Query Store, navigate to `https://learn.microsoft.com/en-us/sql/relational-databases/performance/manage-the-query-store`. For performance tuning using Query Store, navigate to `https://learn.microsoft.com/en-us/sql/relational-databases/performance/tune-performance-with-the-query-store`.

In this section, we covered why establishing baselines is important while listing various client-side tools such as Google Page Speed Insights, Lighthouse, GTMetrix, Google Search Console, and Chrome DevTools for gauging performance. We also looked at server-side tools such as Visual Studio Performance Profiler, Benchmark.net, Application Insights, JetBrains dotMemory and dotTrace, RedGate ANTS Performance Profiler/Memory Profiler, and NDepend for identifying issues with codebases. With databases, we mentioned two tools to identify performance bottlenecks: SQL Server Management Studio Profiler and Query Store. We also mentioned hotspots, or hot paths, where frequently called, unoptimized code could cause performance issues in your application.

The next section will cover the best practices for some client-side and server-side techniques, but will mostly focus on server-side optimizations using C#.

Applying Performance Best Practices

As mentioned at the beginning of this chapter, the content in this chapter applies to client *and* server techniques to get the most out of your ASP.NET websites.

In this section, we'll first focus on optimizing the client by applying image optimization, minimizing your requests, using CDNs, and other tips to improve client-side performance. Then we'll focus on server-side techniques such as optimizing your HTML, caching, and **Entity Framework Core** performance techniques along with identifying slow queries.

Optimizing client-side performance

In this section, we'll learn about image optimizations, identifying Google's **Core Web Vitals** metrics, using a CDN when applicable, how to minimize requests, and where to place scripts and styles.

Fixing Image Optimization

According to the Web Almanac (`https://almanac.httparchive.org/en/2022/media#bytesizes`), image optimization is one of the worst problems on the web. The number of devices required to support it doesn't make this any easier. Let's see how we can optimize this experience.

Here's the basic usage of an `<img>` tag:

```
<img width="100" height="100"
     src="/images/logo.jpg"
     alt="Buck's Coffee Shop Logo"
```

However, for responsive layouts, the `<img>` tag has an `srcset` attribute:

```
<img src="/images/logo-400.jpg"
alt="Buck›s Coffee Shop Logo"
width="100"
height="100"
loading="lazy"
srcset="logo-400.jpg 400w,
logo-800.jpg 800w,
logo-1024.jpg 1024w"
sizes="(max-width: 640px) 400px, 800px, 1024px">
```

The preceding code identifies the size of the viewport (the web page) and loads the appropriate image. The `max-width` media condition says that if the viewport is 640px, use the 400px image. If the max-width is over 640px and less than 800px, use the 800px image.

This allows you to support a number of different responsive layouts. Once you define the layout for your site, images should complement the layout size as well. What does this mean? For every image, you should have an image created for each responsive layout. For example, the preceding default image logo should have three images: `logo-400.jpg`, `logo-800.jpg`, and `logo-1024.jpg`.

Also, the `loading="lazy"` tells the browser to defer loading the images until the browser can determine the size of the viewport to display the proper image.

Finally, images can become extremely large and can contain encoded data such as GPS data when a picture is taken. Compressing an image is the process of removing the extra data, making the image smaller and quicker to load in a browser. This is a server-side task and can be included as a task in your client-side task runner (previously discussed in *Chapter 6*).

The minimum steps for image optimization should look like the following:

1. **Determine the site's responsive layouts** – Identify the sizes you need for your images (400px, 800px, etc.)

2. **Create the images based on the layouts** – There should be a resized image for each layout size.

3. **Optimize the images** – For each image on your site, compress the images so they are smaller and load faster by removing the extra data attached to each image. Use image services such as Optimazilla (`https://imagecompressor.com/`) or TinyPNG (`https://tinypng.com/`).

4. **Add the new <img> attributes** – Each image tag should include the `srcset` and `sizes` attributes so the browser can determine the best image to display based on the viewport size.

Image optimization is too big a topic for a small chapter, but this quick overview should be enough to provide a better experience for website users.

Minimizing requests

Most of the aforementioned client-side tools for creating baselines can be used to identify where multiple requests are made for resources. On average, websites have 58 requests for JavaScript and CSS (that's *not* counting images). Each request causes latency and depending on the resource, it'll take longer than a user is willing to wait.

We've already learned how to use a better approach when structuring your JavaScript and CSS back in *Chapter 6*, eliminating a large number of requests for your JavaScript and CSS files.

Finally, if there's a large number of consistent-sized images and you're calling each one separately, a better approach would be to create one large image (sprite sheet) containing all of the images and use CSS to display them. Instead of your browser requesting 15 social network logos, make one call to an image and split them out using CSS, as shown in *Figure 10.5*:

Figure 10.5 – Sprite sheet of 32x32 social network icons

To use this sprite sheet, the CSS would look like the following:

```
.bg-YouTube_32 {
    width: 32px; height: 32px;
    background: url('css_sprites.png') -1px -1px;
```

```
}
.bg-facebook_32x32 {
    width: 32px; height: 32px;
    background: url('css_sprites.png') -35px -1px;
}
.bg-github_32x32 {
    width: 32px; height: 32px;
    background: url('css_sprites.png') -1px -35px;
}
.bg-Instagram_32 {
    width: 32px; height: 32px;
    background: url('css_sprites.png') -35px -35px;
}
.bg-LinkedIn_32 {
    width: 32px; height: 32px;
    background: url('css_sprites.png') -69px -1px;
}
.bg-quora_32x32 {
    width: 32px; height: 32px;
    background: url('css_sprites.png') -69px -35px;
}
.bg-RSS_32x32 {
    width: 32px; height: 32px;
    background: url('css_sprites.png') -1px -69px;
}
.bg-Twitter_32 {
    width: 32px; height: 32px;
    background: url('css_sprites.png') -35px -69px;
}
```

The background identifies which image to use as a background by using the offset top and left positions. To display the RSS icon in HTML, it would be presented as the following:

```
<div class="bg-RSS_32x32"></div>
```

Such services to create sprites include CodeShack's Images to Sprite Sheet Generator (https://codeshack.io/images-sprite-sheet-generator/) and Toptal's CSS Sprites Generator (https://www.toptal.com/developers/css/sprite-generator).

Using CDNs

If a site uses a large number of static files, using a **content delivery network** (CDN) provides a much-needed service of delivering content based on location. These geographically based servers cache files so they're delivered quicker based on where a user is located.

For example, if someone in California requests a file from Nevada, it's quicker than someone requesting the file from England. The closer the content, the quicker the user receives it.

Final thoughts on client-side performance

While there are a ton of client-side tips we could cover, let's close this section out with some final thoughts on making the client quicker:

- **Scripts at the bottom, styles at the top** – Avoid placing scripts in the header, but absolutely place the styles in the header. Placing scripts at the bottom confirms the **Document Object Model (DOM)** is completely loaded and, if immediately executed, JavaScript is able to find the DOM elements because they've already been rendered.

- **Apply Google's Core Web Vitals to your site** – If you're using either Lighthouse or Google's Page Speed Insights, you'll notice the following acronyms for identifying your site's performance: FCP (First Contentful Paint), LCP (Largest Contentful Paint), CLS (Cumulative Layout Shift), and FID (First Input Delay). Review these terms at `https://web.dev/vitals` to provide a better web experience for your users.

- **Replace JavaScript with HTML** – Sometimes, using simple HTML is better than loading a full-blown JavaScript framework. Case in point, if you need an accordion, the `<details>`/`<summary>` HTML tags may be enough. Also, browsers are becoming even more modern and evolved with new tags such as the `<dialog>` tag where JavaScript isn't necessary. Refer to `https://caniuse.com/` for browser support.

In this section, you learned how to optimize the client side by optimizing your images, along with how CDNs improve the loading of your static content and how to minimize your requests to lower latency issues. For our final notes, we examined some tips such as placing scripts at the bottom and styles at the top, applying Google's Core Web Vitals to websites, providing sites that are responsive regardless of device, and using HTML instead of JavaScript where it makes sense.

In the next section, we'll shift our focus from the client to the server side and look at some of the common practices when optimizing C# and Entity Framework Core.

Common Server-side Practices

With C# being such a robust language, there are so many ways to create a web application. As you saw in *Chapter 5* with Entity Framework Core, each design pattern fit a certain need but worked the same regardless of the pattern. The good news with these performance techniques is they apply to web standards and design patterns already used in the industry. One such example is ETags. At one point, they were considered a separate web concept requiring specific code. Now, when using static files, these ETags are integrated into websites without any additional coding. They're considered a web standard with browsers.

What we're going to address in this section is how to improve performance by adding these web standards and design patterns to our own web application to make it even faster.

In this section, we'll learn about the various performance enhancements we can apply to your code using C#, including quick performance gains you can apply immediately to your own website, and we'll learn how to add a middleware component to optimize your HTML, improve Entity Framework Core performance with only four letters, and identify slow Entity Framework Core queries.

Applying quick performance wins

While some of these quick hits are well-known (and some have been covered in previous chapters), it doesn't hurt to review them to get the most performance out of your website:

- **Turn Debug Off** – When you run your application with debug mode, additional information is compiled into each assembly for debugging purposes. When changed to release mode, you are getting an optimized version of your assemblies for deployment.

- **Use async/await** – As mentioned in previous chapters, using async/await provides performance benefits and should be used for tasks involving file I/O, database, and API calls.

- **Use the database** – When using Entity Framework Core, try to assess the goal and evaluate the best approach: whether it's an Entity Framework Core simple data access method or whether a stored procedure would provide faster performance.

- **Use .AsNoTracking()** – As mentioned in *Chapter 5*, if you have an Entity Framework query not requiring `ChangeState` management such as updating an entity, use `.AsNoTracking()` to reduce the Entity Framework overhead.

While these are some tips to give a web application a quick lift in performance, we're now ready to dive into more involved code-based techniques.

Optimizing the HTML

Since we learned about optimizing images (in the last section) and optimizing JavaScript and CSS (in *Chapter 6*), we now need to focus on the *other* client-side resource: HTML.

When you "view source" in the browser, you'd like to see this beautifully formatted document that everyone can understand. But when the browser receives this document, it doesn't care how big it is or even how "pretty" it is. The browser simply parses and renders the HTML as it comes in.

Have you noticed how much space is wasted in this document for the sake of formatting? For example, let's load the "Buck's Coffee Shop" web page.

In the **Network** tab in Chrome DevTools, we see it's 4.1 KB:

Name	Status	Type	Initiator	Size	Time
📄 localhost	200	document	Other	4.1 kB	44 ms

Figure 10.6 – Approximate size of Buck's Coffee Shop with spaces (4.1 KB)

Since the browser doesn't care, wouldn't it be better if we could reduce the size of the HTML?

Middleware can assist with this. If we use our standard middleware template from *Chapter 2*, we can create an `HtmlShrink` component:

```
public class HtmlShrinkMiddleware
{
    private readonly RequestDelegate _next;

    public HtmlShrinkMiddleware(RequestDelegate next) => _next = next;

    public async Task InvokeAsync(HttpContext context)
    {
        using var buffer = new MemoryStream();

        // Replace the context response with our buffer
        var stream = context.Response.Body;
        context.Response.Body = buffer;

        // Invoke the rest of the pipeline
        // if there are any other middleware components
        await _next(context);

        // Reset and read out the contents
        buffer.Seek(0, SeekOrigin.Begin);

        // Adjust the response stream to remove whitespace.
        var compressedHtmlStream = new HtmlShrinkStream(stream);

        // Reset the stream again
        buffer.Seek(0, SeekOrigin.Begin);

        // Copy our content to the original stream and put it back
        await buffer.CopyToAsync(compressedHtmlStream);
        context.Response.Body = compressedHtmlStream;
    }
}
```

```
public static class HtmlShrinkMiddlewareExtensions
{
    public static IApplicationBuilder UseHtmlShrink(
        this IApplicationBuilder builder)
    {

        return builder.UseMiddleware<HtmlShrinkMiddleware>();

    }

}
```

The preceding code contains our familiar middleware scaffolding. Our HtmlShrinkMiddleware component now instantiates an HtmlShrinkStream class to perform our compression, removing any whitespace in the HTML. Also, we created the standard extension at the bottom of the code.

Our HtmlShrinkStream class is shown in the following:

```
public class HtmlShrinkStream: Stream
{

    private readonly Stream _responseStream;

    public HtmlShrinkStream(Stream responseStream)
    {

        ArgumentNullException.ThrowIfNull(responseStream);

        _responseStream = responseStream;

    }

    public override bool CanRead => _responseStream.CanRead;
    public override bool CanSeek => _responseStream.CanSeek;
    public override bool CanWrite => _responseStream.CanWrite;
    public override long Length => _responseStream.Length;
    public override long Position
    {
        get => _responseStream.Position;
        set => _responseStream.Position = value;
    }

    public override void Flush() => _responseStream.Flush();
    public override int Read(byte[] buffer, int offset, int count) =>
        _responseStream.Read(buffer, offset, count);

    public override long Seek(long offset, SeekOrigin origin) =>
        _responseStream.Seek(offset, origin);
```

```
public override void SetLength(long value) =>
    _responseStream.SetLength(value);

public override void Write(byte[] buffer, int offset, int count)
{
    var html = Encoding.UTF8.GetString(buffer, offset, count);
    var removeSpaces = new Regex(@"(?<=\s)\s+(?![^<>]*</pre>)",
RegexOptions.Multiline);

    html = removeSpaces.Replace(html, string.Empty);
var removeCrLf = new Regex(@"(\r\n|\r|\n)", RegexOptions.Multiline);
html = removeCrLf.Replace(html, string.Empty);

    buffer = Encoding.UTF8.GetBytes(html);

    _responseStream.WriteAsync(buffer, 0, buffer.Length);
}
}
```

In our `HtmlShrinkStream` class, our efforts are concentrated on the `Write()` method. We look at the buffer received, turn it into an HTML string, replace all whitespace by using a RegEx, and finally, write the `buffer` to the `responseStream`.

We can now add our `HtmlShrink` middleware extension to our pipeline by adding the following line to our `Program.cs` file:

```
app.UseHtmlShrink();
```

Once added, any HTML received in the browser will be stripped of any whitespace. If we look at Buck's Coffee Shop home page, we can see everything works, but if we view the source, we can see everything is a little more compact:

Figure 10.7 – Viewing the source of Buck's Coffee Shop home page

It may not look pretty, but if we look at the **Network** tab in Chrome DevTools, we can see a difference in what was sent to the browser:

Name	Status	Type	Initiator	Size	Time	Waterfall
localhost	200	document	Other	3.3 kB	29 ms	

Figure 10.8 – Size of Buck's Coffee Shop home page without spaces (3.3 KB)

That's almost 20% smaller than the original size.

Enabling DbContext pooling

Connection pooling is the ability to reuse a connection for multiple users. By default, database connections already use connection pooling through a `SqlConnection`. This concept was applied to Entity Framework Core's `DbContext`.

If a web application uses Entity Framework Core heavily, you want the best performance available. All it takes is to update your middleware `DbContext` connection.

For example, I might have the following line in my middleware:

```
services.AddDbContext<MyDbContext>(options =>
    options.UseSqlServer(connectionString));
```

We can immediately improve our performance by adding four letters to this line:

```
services.AddDbContextPool<MyDbContext>(options =>
    options.UseSqlServer(connectionString));
```

Using the `AddDbContextPool<>()` method contains the same syntax, but after a `DbContext` is done, it will reset its state and store it for later when a new instance of the `DbContext` is required. We are recycling our `DbContext`s!

Depending on how large your `DbContext` is, every time a new instance is created, the creation of the `DbContext` takes time. Using the `.AddDbContextPool<>()` method gives us the performance boost we need.

Entity Framework Core DbContext pooling benchmarks

Microsoft performed benchmarks with and without DbContext pooling. With DbContext pooling implemented, the performance increased by over 50%. Microsoft even included the source code to the benchmark code. The results can be found at `https://learn.microsoft.com/en-us/ef/core/performance/advanced-performance-topics#benchmarks`.

Identifying slow queries

The ability to identify slow queries is sometimes difficult, since we are in Visual Studio and may not see what's happening behind the scenes when sending a query to the database. So, how do we find these slow queries in our web application?

In the DbContext's `OnConfiguring()` method, add a `.LogTo()` method to your `DbContextOptionsBuilder` and you'll see every database call and the time it took to execute it:

```
protected override void OnConfiguring(DbContextOptionsBuilder
optionsBuilder)
{
    if (!optionsBuilder.IsConfigured)
    {
        var connString = _configuration.
GetConnectionString(«DefaultConnection»);
        if (!string.IsNullOrEmpty(connString))
        {
            optionsBuilder.UseSqlServer(connString)
                .LogTo(Console.WriteLine, LogLevel.Information);
        }
    }
}
```

The `.LogTo()` method will produce the following log entry:

```
Microsoft.EntityFrameworkCore.Database.Command: Information:
Executed DbCommand (46ms) [Parameters=[], CommandType='Text',
CommandTimeout='30']
SELECT [a].[ID], [a].[LocationID], [a].[Name], [l].[ID], [l].[Name]
```

```
FROM [Attractions] AS [a]
INNER JOIN [Locations] AS [l] ON [a].[LocationID] = [l].[ID]
```

For this particular query, it took *46ms* to execute. The `.LogTo()` method provides an easy way to identify whether a query is performing to the best of its ability or is a likely candidate for optimization.

In this section, we learned some bite-sized optimizations along with a new middleware to shrink your HTML, how to speed up Entity Framework Core using DbContext pooling, and how to locate slow queries throughout your application.

In the next section, we'll focus on the various types of caching and how each one is different and can work collectively to improve the overall performance of your application.

Understanding caching

Since caching is extremely important to a web application, it's only fitting it gets its own section to cover all of the possible types of caching available. In the industry, there's a saying: "the best database call is no call at all." They're likely referring to caching.

In this section, we'll learn the different types of caching that include response and output caching, data caching, and caching static files.

Using response caching and output caching

Whether making a call to a web page or an API, the ability to cache data is extremely important. Implementing a simple caching strategy to immediately return data is efficient.

`ResponseCaching` is a middleware extension that is best suited for GET or HEAD API requests from a client. When utilizing response caching, .NET uses the standard HTTP caching semantics.

> **RFC 9111: HTTP caching**
>
> For additional material on HTTP caching, navigate to `https://www.rfc-editor.org/rfc/rfc9111`.

To add response caching, the builder must add it to the services and the application (app) must "use" it, as shown in the following:

```
Var builder = WebApplication.CreateBuilder(args);

builder.Services.AddResponseCaching();

var app = builder.Build();

app.UseHttpsRedirection();
```

```
// If using Cors, UseCors must be placed before the UseResponseCaching
// app.UseCors();

app.UseResponseCaching();
```

Once in place, any API call would provide the cached data from the browser by default.

ResponseCaching middleware

For more details on ResponseCaching, navigate to https://learn.microsoft.com/en-us/aspnet/core/performance/caching/middleware.

However, for most web UIs such as Razor Pages, OutputCaching is the better option because browsers set request headers to prevent caching. OutputCaching's configuration is similar to ResponseCaching, as shown in the following:

```
var builder = WebApplication.CreateBuilder(args);

builder.Services.AddOutputCache();

// Add services to the container.
builder.Services.AddRazorPages();

var app = builder.Build();

// Configure the HTTP request pipeline.
If (!app.Environment.IsDevelopment())
{
    app.UseExceptionHandler("/Error");
    // The default HSTS value is 30 days. You may want to change this
for production scenarios, see https://aka.ms/aspnetcore-hsts.
    App.UseHsts();
}

app.UseHttpsRedirection();
app.UseStaticFiles();

app.UseRouting();

// if using Cors, UseOutputCache must be placed AFTER useCors().
//app.UseCors();

app.UseOutputCache();
```

In the middleware configuration, we add the `AddOutputCache()` method to the services collection and place the `UseOutputCache()` method after the `UseRouting()` method and, if it's used, after the `UseCors()` method.

When the `OutputCache` is added to the middleware, this doesn't mean we are automatically caching our UI pages. We also need to identify which pages are cached by adding an `[OutputCache]` attribute to the Razor Page class:

```
[OutputCache]
public class IndexModel : PageModel
{
    private readonly ILogger<IndexModel> _logger;

    public IndexModel(ILogger<IndexModel> logger)
    {
        _logger = logger;
    }

    public void OnGet() { }
}
```

If no parameters are defined in the attribute, the default policy for caching pages is as follows:

- HTTP 200 status codes are cached
- HTTP GET or HEAD requests are cached
- Responses where cookies are set are *not* cached
- Responses to authenticated requests are *not* cached

Response caching is meant for caching on the client side or through the browser and output caching is cached on the server. If two users access the same page from two different browsers, response caching won't help since each browser will cache the page in each browser. However, if output caching was implemented, this would cache the page on the server and quickly deliver the page to both users.

Caching your pages gives users a better experience when coupled with data caching, which we'll discuss next.

Implementing data caching

When a user visits a website, they are shown a certain amount of data based on who they are. For example, when the first user visits a blog, they could be presented with the same data as the next visitor to the site. If the data doesn't change that often, it doesn't make sense to travel all the way back to the database to retrieve the same data again. Data caching helps us solve this problem. Data caching is taking commonly used data and storing it for a period of time.

Let's look at an example to show the approach. Since we're using Entity Framework Core, we'll have an existing service (`CoffeeService`) containing a simple `.GetAll()` method returning all of the coffees. We can wrap a new caching class around the service called `CacheCoffeeService`, as shown in the following:

```
public class CacheCoffeeService : CoffeeService, ICachedCoffeeService
{
    private const string keyCoffeeList = «EntireCoffeeList»;

    private readonly IMemoryCache _cache;

    public CacheCoffeeService(IBucksDbContext dbContext,
        IMemoryCache cache)
        : base(dbContext)
    {
        _cache = cache;
    }

    public List<Coffee> GetAll(bool reload = false)
    {
        // If we can't find it in the cache or want to reload...
        if (!_cache.TryGetValue(keyCoffeeList, out List<Coffee>
        coffees) || reload)
        {
            coffees = base.GetAll();

            _cache.Set(keyCoffeeList, coffees,
                new MemoryCacheEntryOptions()
                    .SetSlidingExpiration(TimeSpan.FromSeconds(60))
                    // 1min
                    .SetAbsoluteExpiration(TimeSpan.FromSeconds(3600))
                    // 6min
                    .SetPriority(CacheItemPriority.Normal)
            );
        }

        return coffees;
    }
}

public interface ICachedCoffeeService
{
    List<Coffee> GetAll(bool reload = false);
}
```

`CacheCoffeeService` inherits from `CoffeeService` and uses the `ICachedCoffeeService` interface. The `ICachedCoffeeService` interface should be *exactly* the same as `CoffeeService` except for one minor detail: a reload parameter added to each call with a default of false.

If we can't find the entire list of coffees in the cache or we decide we want to reload the entire coffee list, we make a call to the base class (`CoffeeService.GetAll()`)), save the new list to the cache, and return the entire list.

By default, when you call `CachedCoffeeService.GetAll()` with no parameters, you'll get the cached version of the list. Pass a `true` to the `.GetAll()` and you'll refresh your cache and receive the latest list of coffees.

This approach provides the benefit of combining a caching layer with standard data access, giving us the best of both worlds. When creating these data caches, the benefit is immediately obvious: gaining performance by using memory as your database, which is thread-safe. However, be wary of how many tables or how much data you are storing in the cache.

While it may seem like a trade-off using memory as a database, another caching option is using a distributed cache. A distributed cache is a cache shared across multiple app servers and provides the following benefits:

- It is coherent/aware of requests across servers

- If the power goes out for a server, the cached data is persisted

- As mentioned, a distributed cache doesn't use local memory

Some of the best candidates for data caching are small lookup tables (< 100 records) and rarely-accessed table data.

Caching static files

With all of these static files such as images, CSS, and JavaScript available to our web application, you'd think there would be a way to cache these files as well.

In the `.UseStaticFiles()` method, there is a context parameter containing an `HttpContext`, so we can use the response object to change the cache-control headers for our static files:

```
app.UseStaticFiles(new StaticFileOptions
{
    OnPrepareResponse = ctx =>
    {
        // Cached for 24 hours.
        var response = ctx.Context.Response;
        var duration = 60 * 60 * 24; // 24h duration.
        response.Headers[HeaderNames.CacheControl] =
        "public,max-age="+duration;
```

```
    }
});
```

The preceding code takes our static files middleware component and allows a `StaticFileOptions` instance, which also has an `OnPrepareResponse` event available to us. For our cache duration, we set every static file header's cache duration to 24 hours.

If we wanted to disable caching, we would modify the response to change the following headers:

```
app.UseStaticFiles(new StaticFileOptions
{
    OnPrepareResponse = ctx =>
    {
        var response = ctx.Context.Response;
        // disable all caching
        response.Headers[HeaderNames.CacheControl] = "no-cache,
            no-store";
        response.Headers[HeaderNames.Pragma] = "no-cache";
        response.Headers[HeaderNames.Expires] = "-1";


    }
});
```

The preceding code sample disables caching for every static file.

Again, while these files are cached on the server's local memory, keep in mind that when the power goes down, so does the cache.

If you wanted to cache a certain folder or file type, the `ctx` parameter contains not only a `Context` property of the `HttpContext` type, but a `File` property containing an `IFileInfo` type that includes `FileInfo` data.

Summary

While we covered a lot in this chapter, there are additional ways to achieve performance in web applications using more advanced techniques. The methods covered in this chapter are the best approaches for achieving performance in ASP.NET web applications. More than ever, performance is now considered one of the more important features in web applications, since it's now usually tied to a company's finances.

In this chapter, we first learned why performance matters by showing the effects of a slow website, how minor adjustments can produce large dividends, and how search engines reward websites for performance improvements.

We learned how to create baselines to identify possible bottlenecks using performance tools to analyze the client and server-side code with various tools.

Then, we learned about client-side techniques to optimize images, using CDNs to improve the loading of static content, and how to minimize your requests to lower latency issues. We also examined some quick tips such as placing scripts at the bottom and styles at the top, reviewing Google's Core Web Vitals to understand how they gauge website performance, and using HTML instead of JavaScript where it's relevant.

Finally, we focused on the server side by reviewing some small, immediate optimizations along with improving performance by optimizing HTML before it's sent back to the client. From there, we learned how to speed up Entity Framework Core by adding DbContext pooling and identifying slow queries. The final piece to our performance chapter was implementing caching, which included learning about response caching, output caching, data caching, and how to cache static files.

In the appendix, we'll examine some programming guidelines, along with what ASP.NET 8 projects look like nowadays.

11
Appendix

When writing code, every language has its nuances and standards. .NET is no different when it comes to general guidelines. One example is that placing a bracket at the end of a method signature is better than placing the bracket on the next line or placing a return immediately on the same line as an `if` statement. This is more of a personal preference. Programming guidelines give developers a way to stay between guardrails while writing code. These programming guidelines are used throughout the industry as standard practices.

In the appendix, we're going to cover the following main topics:

- Programming guidelines
- Project structure

The guidelines discussed in the following sections are commonly used in the industry. They give developers direction and provide guardrails as to how one should structure and write code not only for themselves, but also for other developers and peers in the future (including our future selves).

In the first section, we'll review some programming guidelines such as the DRY, YAGNI, and KISS principles, along with separation of concerns, the concept of SOLID, and how refactoring is a process and not a one-time quick fix. We'll finish the appendix by looking at recommended ways of organizing .NET projects and folder structures, and where code resides based on their function.

Technical requirements

The only technical requirement for the appendix is access to your editor since we'll be covering general programming guidelines. While we will have snippets of code along the way, they don't justify their own code repository. They're only meant to solidify the understanding of the concepts.

Programming guidelines

Throughout the book, I recommend various intermediate and advanced techniques of writing code pertaining to a particular topic or technology. While these techniques are meant to give developers a balance between requirements and technologies, there is also a need to provide common programming guidelines to follow certain patterns, making it easier for colleagues and peers to understand a code base. Successful developers think about these guidelines while writing and maintaining code.

In this section, we'll review the DRY, YAGNI, KISS, and SOLID principles along with understanding separation of concerns, and how refactoring is a process.

DRY

The first acronym we'll review is probably one of the simplest guidelines to follow. The **DRY** principle stands for **don't repeat yourself**.

If you have multiple methods performing the same task in different locations of your application, it may be time to refactor and consolidate the code.

YAGNI

Our next common acronym is **YAGNI** (pronounced yag-nee), which stands for **you aren't gonna need it**.

Also referred to as "building the bridge to nowhere," the concept behind this acronym is to let developers know they should only write code when there is a requirement for it. They shouldn't add code for a possible future enhancement that may not come to fruition.

KISS

Since this next acronym has so many meanings, we'll try to keep it simple (hence the name). **KISS** stands for **keep it simple, stupid**.

```
Albert Einstein mentioned "Make everything as simple as possible, but
not simpler," and Steve Jobs of Apple always said, "Simplify."
```

Keep your units of code simple enough to understand. This can include the following:

- **Smaller methods** – The smaller the method, the easier it is to read and understand

- **Language enhancements** – Based on .NET's C# language improvements over the years, there may be a better (and shorter) way to write code

- **Reducing complexity** – When reducing complexity, systems become more testable and can be a possible candidate for automated testing

The goal is to build more value by creating a better code base for peers and colleagues.

Separation of concerns

When you started writing your own application, running it and seeing it execute on the screen for the first time was a huge achievement.

Over time, the application required a database. Then it required email capabilities. Then logging. Then authentication. The requirements grew and so on and so on.

The separation of concerns concept pertains to how you logically partition an application into distinct layers. For example, if an application requires an email module, it would be a separate project in the solution called `MyApplication.EmailModule`. This email module would provide the following benefits to the application:

- **Modularization** – `EmailModule` could be reused in another application if necessary.

- **Encapsulation** – `EmailModule` doesn't require any outside dependencies; it's self-contained.

- **Testable** – If everything is contained inside `EmailModule`, unit testing (and possibly integration testing) becomes easier.

- **Maintainability** – This allows developers to focus only on `EmailModule` as opposed to the entire application. When focusing on one particular section, it doesn't require the knowledge of the entire application. The knowledge of the project is all that's required.

One of the concepts heard in the industry is "Big Ball of Mud." This concept pertains to all of the application code contained in one project, which is an unmaintainable code base. This is a similar concept to a "monolith," where the application is hard to maintain because of its size. Consequently, concepts in the application aren't broken out into modular units of work. If everything in the application is coupled together…everywhere, the system is brittle. If a developer modifies code in one location, it may fix the current issue but it will introduce errors in other locations, causing a ripple effect throughout the entire code base.

Separation of concerns is something that experienced developers should share with their peers through code reviews to improve software on a larger scale and provide healthy discussions on the topic.

Refactoring as a process

While refactoring is a fundamental concept for developers, there are various levels of effort involved in refactoring a code base.

One simple example could be the renaming of a method. Once a developer renames a method, the developer has to change all of the references to that method in the code base. A more advanced example is the refactoring of a business rules engine to create more flexibility. While both are refactoring, one is easier than the other.

Refactoring should be a process. One process I've used over the years is as follows:

- **Get it functional** – Write functional code that works
- **Get it tested** – Create tests to confirm the code behaves as expected
- **Get it refactored** – Refactor and optimize the code

The code you write should (usually) have tests (see the "100% Test Coverage" myth in *Chapter 7*).

With that said, if you're going to refactor code, *it will be beneficial to have tests in place* to confirm your refactoring efforts aren't in vain. Once you have tests in place, you are free to refactor and modify as much code as needed to achieve your intended goal.

The business rules engine was an example in my career where the code was functional and a lot of tests were in place (~700 passed). However, the team ran into an issue where the code required a more flexible approach and it had to be refactored. Two team members took three days to refactor the code. Once they finished the refactoring, they ran the final unit tests and found only two failed unit tests. The two failed unit tests were because they didn't rename a method name properly. Imagine this refactoring without the tests.

Refactoring can be as complex or as simple as the code base allows. Always keep in mind that refactoring is a multi-step process and requires tests to confirm the refactored code works as expected.

> **Book recommendation**
>
> One book I would highly recommend is *Refactoring with C#, Matt Eland, Packt Publishing*, available at `https://www.packtpub.com/`.

SOLID principles

SOLID principles provide even deeper guidelines for writing code. SOLID is an acronym and was created back in 2000 by Robert C. Martin.

Over the years, the SOLID principles have become a standard for writing quality software, and give developers a way to gauge their code based on whether it meets each principle's criteria. Developers may disagree with what constitutes SOLID code, but again, these discussions should be had with peers or in a team meeting.

Single responsibility principle

The **single responsibility principle** (SRP) dictates that a class should have one and only one reason to change.

The following code violates the SRP:

```
public class User
{
    public string Name { get; set; }
    public string Email { get; set; }
    public bool IsValid()
    {
        // Validate the user data here
        if (string.IsNullOrEmpty(Name) || string.IsNullOrEmpty(Email))
        {
            return false;
        }
        return true;
    }
    public void Save()
    {
        // Save user data to database here
    }
}
```

The User class has two properties: Name and Email. However, we have extra methods performing other responsibilities: an IsValid() method and a Save() method. Our User class is doing more than it should. We should create two new classes: one called UserValidation for validation, and one called UserService or UserRepository for database operations.

We created two additional classes but provided better software composition. If we add a new property to the User class and it requires validation, the developer only needs to make a change in one place: the UserValidation class.

Open/closed

The **open/closed principle** describes how software components should be open for extension but closed for modification.

Most violations of the open/closed principle are usually indicated by long branching statements (such as long if..then or switch statements).

The following code provides an example:

```
public class ComicBook
{
    public string Title { get; set; } = string.Empty;
    public string Issue { get; set; } = string.Empty;
    public decimal Grading { get; set; }
```

```
public string GetGradeName() =>
    Grading switch
    {
        10.0m => "Gem Mint",
        9.9m => "Mint",
        9.8m => "NM/M",
        >= 9.6m => "NM+",
        >= 9.4m => "NM",
        >= 9.2m => "NM-",
        >= 9.0m => "VF/NM",
        >= 8.5m => "VF+",
        >= 8.0m => "VF",
        >= 7.5m => "VF-",
        >= 7.0m => "FN/VF",
        >= 6.5m => "FN+",
        >= 6.0m => "FN",
        >= 5.5m => "FN-",
        >= 5.0m => "VG/FN",
        >= 4.5m => "VG+",
        >= 4.0m => "VG",
        >= 3.5m => "VG-",
        >= 3.0m => "G/VG",
        >= 2.0m => "G",
        >= 1.8m => "G-",
        >= 1.5m => "Fa/G",
        >= 1.0m => "Fa",
        _ => "Poor"
    };
}
```

In this ComicBook class, we have three properties called Title, Issue, and Grading. One of the requirements for our class is to return the grading name based on the Grading property. This violates the open/closed principle.

Why? Even though we already have the complete list of grades, the **Certified Guaranty Company (CGC)** may rename the grading name in the future to something else. If we wanted to add a new grade name, we would have to go into the GetGradeName() method and add a new grade and name.

A better implementation to support the open/closed principle is as follows:

```
public class Grade
{
    public decimal Value { get; }
```

```
    public string Name { get; }
    private Grade(decimal value, string name)
    {
        Value = value;
        Name = name;
    }
    public static Grade FromDecimal(decimal value) =>
        value switch
        {
            10.0m => new Grade(value, "Gem Mint"),
            9.9m => new Grade(value, "Mint"),
            9.8m => new Grade(value, "NM/M"),
            >= 9.6m => new Grade(value, "NM+"),
            >= 9.4m => new Grade(value, "NM"),
            >= 9.2m => new Grade(value, "NM-"),
            >= 9.0m => new Grade(value, "VF/NM"),
            >= 8.5m => new Grade(value, "VF+"),
            >= 8.0m => new Grade(value, "VF"),
            >= 7.5m => new Grade(value, "VF-"),
            >= 7.0m => new Grade(value, "FN/VF"),
            >= 6.5m => new Grade(value, "FN+"),
            >= 6.0m => new Grade(value, "FN"),
            >= 5.5m => new Grade(value, "FN-"),
            >= 5.0m => new Grade(value, "VG/FN"),
            >= 4.5m => new Grade(value, "VG+"),
            >= 4.0m => new Grade(value, "VG"),
            >= 3.5m => new Grade(value, "VG-"),
            >= 3.0m => new Grade(value, "G/VG"),
            >= 2.0m => new Grade(value, "G"),
            >= 1.8m => new Grade(value, "G-"),
            >= 1.5m => new Grade(value, "Fa/G"),
            >= 1.0m => new Grade(value, "Fa"),
            _ => new Grade(value, "Poor")
        };
}
public class ComicBook
{
    public string Title { get; set; } = string.Empty;
    public string Issue { get; set; } = string.Empty;
    public Grade Grading { get; set; }
}
```

While it looks like we simply moved the switch statement, we did something else. We created a Grade class.

With a `Grade` class created, we can assign any type of grade to the `ComicBook` class. If a new grade type is created, we can easily add it to our list without modifying the `ComicBook` class. We also implemented a factory pattern in our code.

Before, we were comparing a string based on a decimal value. Now, if additional properties are required for a grade, we can extend our `Grade` class to include more information.

Open for extension, closed to modification.

Liskov substitution

The **Liskov substitution principle** explains that any derived type can be replaced with its base types. The concept behind the Liskov substitution is based on inherited types and/or interfaces.

To continue with our comic book example, the following code shows a simple `BasePublisher` class:

```
public class MyNewPublisher : BasePublisher
{
    public MyNewPublisher(): base(nameof(MyNewPublisher)) { }
}

public class BasePublisher
{
    public string Name { get; set; }
    protected BasePublisher(string name)
    {
        Name = name;
    }
    public Address GetAddress()
    {
        return Address.Empty;
    }
}

public class Address
{
    public static Address Empty => new();
    public string Address1 { get; set; } = string.Empty;
    public string Address2 { get; set; } = string.Empty;
    public string City { get; set; } = string.Empty;
    public string State { get; set; } = string.Empty;
    public string ZipCode { get; set; } = string.Empty;
}
```

The `BasePublisher` class contains the name and address of a publisher. When we create a new publisher (such as the preceding `MyNewPublisher` class), we'll have access to everything available in the base class.

The ability to replace a `BasePublisher` class with a `MyNewPublisher` class would be an example of the Liskov substitution principle.

Interface segregation

The **interface segregation principle** explains that clients shouldn't be forced to implement unnecessary methods they won't use.

With every interface created in an application, each method and property defined should be implemented in a concrete class. The defined interfaces should not go to waste in an implementation.

For example, let's say we have an interface for our `ComicBook` class. The interface and implementation code are listed as follows:

```
public interface IComicBook
{
    string Title { get; set; }
    string Issue { get; set; }
    string Publisher { get; set; }
    void SaveToDatabase();
}
public class ComicBook : IComicBook
{
    public string Title { get; set; }
    public string Issue { get; set; }
    public string Publisher { get; set; }
    public void SaveToDatabase()
    {
        throw new NotImplementedException();
    }
}
```

Everything in our `ComicBook` class is justified except for the `SaveToDatabase()` method. Creating a new `ComicBook` instance suggests we'll be using the database every time. This violates the interface segregation principle.

A better implementation would be splitting the database access out into an `IComicBookWriter` with a `SaveToDatabase()` method, as shown in the following code:

```
public interface IComicBook
{
    string Title { get; set; }
```

```
        string Issue { get; set; }
        string Publisher { get; set; }
    }


    public interface IComicBookWriter
    {
        void SaveToDatabase();
    }


    public class ComicBook : IComicBook, IComicBookWriter
    {
        public string Title { get; set; }
        public string Issue { get; set; }
        public string Publisher { get; set; }

        public void SaveToDatabase()
        {
            // Implementation
        }
    }
```

The example code shows how inheriting from the IComicBookWriter gives the ComicBook class a way to persist the data.

The goal of the interface segregation principle is to avoid including methods in an interface that you won't use.

This example is also a violation of the SRP since this class is also accessing the database.

Dependency inversion

The **dependency inversion principle** explains that we should depend on abstractions and not on concrete implementations. With .NET, dependency injection is available out of the box. With dependency injection automatically available, this satisfies half of our dependency inversion principle.

While we can dependency-inject concrete classes into constructors, a better implementation would be to create an interface for the concrete implementation. Using interfaces encourages loose coupling throughout our code base.

For example, back in *Chapter 5* with Entity Framework, we created a simple interface for our DbContexts for this very reason. Instead of registering a concrete implementation of a DbContext, we could use its interface instead.

We registered our abstraction (interface) to support our dependency inversion principle.

In this section, the terms DRY, YAGNI, and KISS, along with what separation of concerns means and how refactoring is a process and not a single task. We finished the section by learning each SOLID practice, namely the single responsibility, open/closed, Liskov substitution, interface segregation, and dependency inversion principles.

In the next section, we'll learn about folder organization based on project types.

Project structure

As mentioned in *Chapter 7*, on testing, folder structures can reveal an application's intent and provide documentation as well.

In this section, we'll learn about folder structures with ASP.NET web applications. We'll also learn where to place code based on intent, such as where to place API code or Entity Framework code.

Understanding the project landscape

Every project has its own structure based on its type. For example, a **Razor Page** project layout is different from a **Model-View-Controller** (**MVC**) project or an API project.

Let's examine what folders are in these common projects.

First, the following is an example of an ASP.NET Razor Page project:

Figure 11.1 – Common folder structure of a Razor Page project

Next is an example of an ASP.NET MVC project:

Figure 11.2 - Common folder structure of an MVC project

As we move through each project, we'll explain what each folder does and its purpose in the application.

wwwroot folder

In either of the preceding project types, the `wwwroot` folder contains all of our static content used on the website. Any folder added to this directory is static content and visible to the browser.

One example is an images folder. If we added an images folder to the `wwwroot` folder, the URL to that images folder would look like the following:

```
https://localhost:xxx/images/funnyimage.jpg
```

For JavaScript frameworks (such as Angular, React, etc.), a folder called `source` or `src` should be created under the `wwwroot` folder to hold your client-side source code. The JavaScript framework should be transpiled to another folder of your choosing, such as a `js` or `app` folder for public browser consumption. We touched on these folders in *Chapter 6* when we were building our client-side tasks using a task runner.

Pages folder

In a Razor Page project, the Pages folder is where server-side pages are found. Every folder created is a path to a page.

For example, if we created a Setup folder and added an Index.cshtml file, the URL to execute and view that page would look like the following:

```
https://localhost:xxx/setup/
```

Other folders created under the Pages directory would follow the same path, as shown in *Figure 11.3*:

Figure 11.3 – Folder structure for a MenuManager page

Based on the directory structure in *Figure 11.3*, the URL to **MenuManager** would be as follows:

```
https://localhost:xxx/setup/menumanager/
```

The simpler the folder structure, the easier it is to locate a page and identify page functionality.

Shared folder

The Shared folder is used for common components such as layout pages, ViewComponents, partials, EditorTemplates, and DisplayTemplates. These shared components are accessible through web pages in the Pages folder (if it's a Razor Pages project) or the Views folder (if it's an MVC project).

Controllers folder

MVC projects always contain a `Controllers` folder and are the traffic cops of the web application.

The MVC web model uses a "convention over configuration" concept where the name of the controller is the path and the methods inside the controller class are the page names.

For example, in the aforementioned `Controllers` folder, we have a class called `HomeController`. If we look in `HomeController`, we'll see a method called `Index()`:

```
public class HomeController : Controller
{
    public IActionResult Index()
    {
        return View();
    }
}
```

The presence of a `HomeController` class tells us three things:

- We will have a `/Home` URL with an `Index()` method for a default page
- A Home folder is located under the `/Views` folder
- Since there is an `Index()` method in `HomeController`, there should be an `Index.cshtml` in the `/Views/Home` directory

The `Index()` method tells us when the `https://localhost:xxx/Home` URL is called. It will automatically hit this `Index()` method and, by default, look for the Index view in the `/Views/Home` directory.

Feature folders

One of the secrets of an MVC application is the ability to move controllers around to any folder inside the application. On initial startup, the ASP.NET framework locates all of the controllers available throughout the application and creates a routing table for incoming web requests. Based on this approach, developers in the community have created **feature folders**.

Feature folders are usually contained in a folder called `/Features` off the root with folders underneath to identify the feature implemented. While a `/Features` folder is the most common, developers have the ability to name the folder anything they want. They can also place controllers under any folder in the project. ASP.NET can locate all of the controllers on startup.

These folders usually contain a minimum of a controller, a ViewModel, and a View. They can also contain supporting classes related to the feature. The folder is named based on the feature being implemented.

For example, if there was an image viewing feature in your MVC application, it would look like *Figure 11.4*:

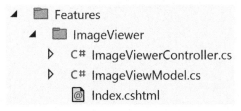

Figure 11.4 – Example of an ImageViewer feature folder

This folder structure provides the following benefits:

- **Focus** – Each feature is isolated so team members can build the feature without causing merge issues

- **Consolidation** – Instead of moving from one folder to another throughout the entire project, features are confined to one folder, making the coding process more efficient

- **Immediate visibility** – If someone said there was an issue in the Accounts Receivable feature, the developer would know to immediately look in the `Features/AccountsReceiveable` folder

In MVC, the View path can be modified to fit your needs. In this case, defining a custom path to your views provides even more flexible configurations for your application.

The `Features` folder technique is becoming a more viable option for creating scalable, feature-based web applications by offering vertical slicing. Vertical slicing is the process of writing code for an entire feature across all layers (presentation, domain, and data access). Feature folders simplify this process and convey isolated features in the application.

Models folder

The `Models` folder contains all of the models used for your Views. This is different from a ViewModel. The difference between Models and ViewModels is that ViewModels are passed into the View and can contain models to support the ViewModel.

An example of a ViewModel is shown in the following code snippet:

```
public class HomeController : Controller
{
    public IActionResult Index()
    {
        return View(new IndexViewModel
        {
            Title = "Home Page",
```

```
            Product = new ProductDto
            {
                Name = "Sunglasses",
                Price = 9.99m
            }
        });
    }
}
public class IndexViewModel
{
    public string Title { get; set; }
    public ProductDto Product { get; set; }
}

public class ProductDto
{
    public string Name { get; set; }
    public decimal Price { get; set; }
}
```

A ViewModel is sent to the View (`IndexViewModel`) where a Model can be data supporting the ViewModel (`ProductDto`).

Two common practices include either creating a `ViewModels` directory under the `Models` folder, or a `ViewModels` directory in the root of your project.

Views folder

In an MVC project, the `Views` folder is the equivalent of the `Pages` folder in a Razor Pages project. It contains the same folder structure as a Razor Pages project.

Creating project layers

When creating a new web application, the default web project contains the bare essentials to run in a browser. But how do you segment the application so you don't have a huge pile of unmanageable code?

A layer, or tier, is a segment of the application broken up into modules or projects designed to perform in a certain way. A presentation layer contains the user interface of how the user interacts with the website, while a data access layer retrieves data for the application.

Identifying project layers can be a bit of a daunting task, but the best way is to create application layers based on their functionality. Each project will have a consistent naming convention based on its function.

While the following are recommended project layers and names, architect and team suggestions may overrule these choices:

- **Core domain/business rules** – The domain or business rules project should be at the core of your application. These projects are usually named `<ProjectName>.Domain` or `<ProjectName>.Core`.

- **User interface (UI)** – The UI is already available when creating the initial web application through **File | New | ASP.NET Web Application**. The recommended naming convention for these projects could be `<ProjectName>.Web` or `<ProjectName>.UI`.

- **Databases** – Database access should be contained in `<ProjectName>.Data` or `<ProjectName>.Infrastructure`.

- **APIs** – APIs should be in their own folder (`/api`) or contained in a separate project called `<ProjectName>.Api`.

- **Services** – Services is another layer encapsulating higher-level functions. While this is an optional layer and these types of services could be located inside the `Infrastructure` project, the amount of code in an infrastructure project can become overwhelming. A services project could provide an alternative to the `Infrastructure` project. Services could include a `MailService` or `<Entity>Service`. These projects are usually named `<ProjectName>.Services`.

These code layers provide the best layout when organizing your project. Each project name describes the intent and gives developers a clear representation of the solution as a whole.

Summary

In this appendix, we learned the DRY, YAGNI, and KISS principles, along with separation of concerns, the concept of SOLID, and how refactoring is a process and not a one-time quick fix.

We proceeded to look at how two common ASP.NET web applications were structured and what each folder represented. Once we understood a project's folder structure, we examined where code would reside based on its intent, such as Entity Framework or service classes.

Thank you!

Best practices are considered to be what is correct, common, and accepted by others in the field. The best practices contained in this book are a combination of observations, experience, and feedback over the years from my peers, mentors, and the developer community.

I hope these best practices serve as a reference for your ASP.NET development career and that you can achieve the same level of excitement as I do when I experience a new programming technique or technology.

Thank you for your readership!

Code on, developers... code on!

Index

www.packtpub.com

Subscribe to our online digital library for full access to over 7,000 books and videos, as well as industry leading tools to help you plan your personal development and advance your career. For more information, please visit our website.

Why subscribe?

- Spend less time learning and more time coding with practical eBooks and Videos from over 4,000 industry professionals

- Improve your learning with Skill Plans built especially for you

- Get a free eBook or video every month

- Fully searchable for easy access to vital information

- Copy and paste, print, and bookmark content

Did you know that Packt offers eBook versions of every book published, with PDF and ePub files available? You can upgrade to the eBook version at packtpub.com and as a print book customer, you are entitled to a discount on the eBook copy. Get in touch with us at customercare@packtpub.com for more details.

At www.packtpub.com, you can also read a collection of free technical articles, sign up for a range of free newsletters, and receive exclusive discounts and offers on Packt books and eBooks.

Other Books You May Enjoy

If you enjoyed this book, you may be interested in these other books by Packt:

Architecting ASP.NET Core Applications

Carl-Hugo Marcotte

ISBN: 978-1-80512-338-5

- Apply the SOLID principles for building flexible and maintainable software
- Test your apps effectively with automated tests, including black-box testing
- Enter the path of ASP.NET Core dependency injection mastery
- Work with GoF design patterns such as strategy, decorator, facade, and composite
- Design REST APIs using Minimal APIs and MVC
- Discover layering techniques and the tenets of clean architecture
- Use feature-oriented techniques as an alternative to layering
- Explore microservices, CQRS, REPL, vertical slice architecture, and many more patterns

Apps and Services with .NET 8

Mark J. Price

ISBN: 978-1-83763-713-3

- Get familiar with a variety of technologies for implementing services, like gRPC and GraphQL
- Store and manage data locally and cloud native with SQL Server and Cosmos DB
- Use ADO.NET SqlClient for implementing web services with native AOT publish support
- Leverage Dapper for improved performance over EF Core
- Implement popular third-party libraries like Serilog, FluentValidation, Humanizr, and Noda Time
- Explore the new unified hosting model of Blazor Full Stack

Packt is searching for authors like you

If you're interested in becoming an author for Packt, please visit `authors.packtpub.com` and apply today. We have worked with thousands of developers and tech professionals, just like you, to help them share their insight with the global tech community. You can make a general application, apply for a specific hot topic that we are recruiting an author for, or submit your own idea.

Share Your Thoughts

Now you've finished *ASP.NET 8 Best Practices*, we'd love to hear your thoughts! Scan the QR code below to go straight to the Amazon review page for this book and share your feedback or leave a review on the site that you purchased it from.

`https://packt.link/r/1-837-63480-7`

Your review is important to us and the tech community and will help us make sure we're delivering excellent quality content.

Download a free PDF copy of this book

Thanks for purchasing this book!

Do you like to read on the go but are unable to carry your print books everywhere? Is your eBook purchase not compatible with the device of your choice?

Don't worry, now with every Packt book you get a DRM-free PDF version of that book at no cost.

Read anywhere, any place, on any device. Search, copy, and paste code from your favorite technical books directly into your application.

The perks don't stop there, you can get exclusive access to discounts, newsletters, and great free content in your inbox daily

Follow these simple steps to get the benefits:

1. Scan the QR code or visit the link below

https://packt.link/free-ebook/978-1-83763-212-1

2. Submit your proof of purchase
3. That's it! We'll send your free PDF and other benefits to your email directly

Printed in Great Britain
by Amazon

36207367R00143